FROM THE TERRORISTS' POINT OF VIEW

FROM THE TERRORISTS' POINT OF VIEW

What They Experience and Why They Come to Destroy

Fathali M. Moghaddam

PRAEGER SECURITY INTERNATIONAL
Westport, Connecticut • London

Library of Congress Cataloging-in-Publication Data

Moghaddam, Fathali M.
  From the terrorists' point of view : what they experience and why they come to
  destroy / Fathali M. Moghaddam.
    p. cm.
  Includes bibliographical references and index.
  ISBN 0–275–98825–2 (alk. paper)
    1. Terrorism—United States—Prevention.   2. Islamic fundamentalism—United
States.   3. Terrorism—Religious aspects—Islam.   4. Islam and politics—United States.
5. Terrorism—Psychological aspects.   I. Title.
  HV6432.M62   2006
  363.325–dc22   2006015400

British Library Cataloguing in Publication Data is available

Library of Congress Catalog Card Number: 2006015400
ISBN: 0–275–98825–2

First published in 2006

Praeger Security International, 88 Post Road West, Westport, CT 06881
An imprint of Greenwood Publishing Group, Inc.
www.praeger.com

Printed in the United States of America

The paper used in this book complies with the
Permanent Paper Standard issued by the National
Information Standards Organization (Z39.48–1984).

10 9 8 7 6 5 4 3 2 1

This book is dedicated to victims of terrorism, everywhere.

CONTENTS

PREFACE

I wrote this book in order to explain why Islamic terrorism threatens to continue to be a major global problem, and even grow in strength, well into the twenty-first century. For some groups of Muslims, terrorism is becoming a "normal" response to what they see to be injustice. Why is this? Are these people pathological? Are they illiterate? Ignorant? Do they have abnormal personalities? Are they economically deprived? I argue that these are not at all satisfactory explanations; the real reasons for Islamic terrorism have little to do with these and other characteristics of individual terrorists, but everything to do with a deep crisis of identity.

Islamic communities in many parts of the world are experiencing a profound and historic identity crisis, one tragic manifestation of which is terrorism. In order to understand and avert this destructive trend, we must come to grips with the monumental crisis of identity that is paralyzing moderate movements but energizing fanatic forces in Islamic communities.

Why "from the terrorists' point of view"? Why do we need to understand how the terrorists see the world? Because this is the best way for us to find an effective means to end terrorism. So far we have looked at the world from the point of view of the civilian victims of terrorism, the security forces fighting terrorism, the millions of ordinary people who directly or indirectly witness terrorism, the journalists and documentary makers who report on terrorism, the politicians who legislate in order to try to control terrorism—from just about every angle, except the point of view of terrorists. Seeing the world from the terrorists' point of view does not mean condoning terrorism; rather, it means better understanding terrorism so as to end it.

My understanding of "the terrorists' point of view" came about through three main avenues. A first avenue is direct personal experience of the contexts and cultural systems giving rise to Islamic terrorism. This includes five years of research in post-revolution Iran, projects with Afghan refugees, and interactions with Islamic forces fighting the Soviet invasion of Afghanistan. The mixture of Saudi-funded Salafists, Iran-backed Shi'a extremists, covert American intervention, and local Afghan and Pakistani politics, proved to be far too explosive for the Soviets to handle. But this potent force did not dissipate after the defeat of the Soviets, and it eventually evolved and gave rise to the tragedy of September 11. A second influence on how I see "the terrorists' point of view," is an in-depth study of what captured terrorists have reported, as well as literature on terrorist lives. Third, my understanding of "the terrorists' point of view" is based on my over quarter of a century of research on group and intergroup dynamics, and particularly the role of identity in intergroup conflict.

At the outset, let me make my orientation clear. I believe it is not to individual but to societal characteristics that we must look to understand and to end terrorism. We must pay attention to the "big picture" and the cultural conditions that give rise to a morality supportive of terrorism. We must give priority to transforming these cultural conditions. My intention is to highlight a need for long-term policies to transform social, economic, and political conditions.

Unfortunately Westerners in general and Americans in particular tend to have a blind spot when it comes to appreciating the power of context, and how certain conditions make it inevitable that some individuals will engage in evil acts, including terrorism. Cultures that espouse an ideology of individualism, America supreme among them, find it difficult to appreciate or even acknowledge the power of context. On the surface, this is because the American dream is about individual responsibility and self-help: there seems to be no place for the power of context in the American dream. But at a deeper level, it is a particular context that gives rise to the American dream, just as it is to the context we must look to explain terrorism.

The main focus of my discussion is terrorism arising out of Islamic communities, in both Western and non-Western societies. This is not because I believe all terrorism has religious roots or that terrorism in non-Muslim societies has come to an end, but because I see the main challenge for antiterrorist forces in the next few decades to arise out of the social, political, and economic conditions associated with the identity crisis of Islamic communities. These conditions are giving rise to terrorists with a variety of motives—secular, religious, nationalist, and ethnic—but with a common morality that justifies any and every means to achieve their espoused goals.

In the fight to shape the future identity of Islamic societies, fundamentalists are violently and vehemently trying to push Muslims back into an imagined glorious past, and a variety of reformers are struggling to push these societies toward different hoped-for futures. Terrorism is a strategic weapon in these turbulent struggles, and the eye of the storm has shifted to Iraq, where invading armies grapple with entrenched insurgents.

Iraq in particular is proving to be a fertile training ground, even more potent than Pakistan, Afghanistan, and Saudi Arabia, for a new breed of international terrorists, who in the second decade of the twenty-first century will fan out and spread terrorist networks and techniques in numerous Near and Middle Eastern countries, as well as in Western Europe and the rest of the world. The new breed of terrorists number in the tens of thousands and their dispersion from Iraq to the rest of the world will radically alter the dynamics of forces engaged in the so-called "war on terror."

ACKNOWLEDGMENTS

I am grateful to Dennis Smith and Allen Zerkin for organizing a very forward looking set of meetings at the Robert F. Wagner Graduate School of Public Service, New York University, and to the following for instructing me about policies, strategies, conflict, and solutions to terrorism at those meetings: John Brademas (President Emeritus, New York University), Rebecca Horsewell (Chatham House), Mary Knapp (the Fredenberg Initiative), David Little (Harvard University), John McDonald (Institute for Multi-Track Diplomacy), Mohammad Mahmoud Ould Mohamedou (Harvard University), Joseph Montville (George Mason University), Ebrahim Moosa (Duke University), Edward Nell (New School University), Mustapha Tlili (New York University), and Harlan Ullman (Center for Strategic and International Studies).

In recent years I have been involved in numerous informal discussions and formal meetings on the nature of terrorism, and the following are some of the people who have directly or indirectly influenced this book: Salman Akhtar (Jefferson Medical College), Karen Armstrong (author, London, U.K.), Johanna Bockman (George Mason University), Dan Byman (Georgetown University), Natana DeLong-Bas (Boston College), Robin Fox (Rutgers University), Marc Gopin (George Mason University), Johannes Jansen (Leiden University), Philip Jenkins (Penn State University), Douglas Johnston (International Center for Religion and Diplomacy), Edward Luttwak (Center for Strategic and International Studies), Peter Mandaville (George Mason University), Jean-Prancois Layer (Religioscope), Anthony Marsella (University of Hawaii), Clark McCauley (Bryn Mawr College), Timothy McDaniel (University of California, San Diego), Carolyn Nordstrom (University of Notre

Dame), John Peterson (The Arlington Institute), David Rapaport (University of California, Los Angeles), Roland Robertson (University of Aberdeen), Rich Rubenstein (George Mason University), Linda Seligman (George Mason University), Lionel Tiger (Rutgers University), and Vamik Volkan (University of Virginia).

I am, as always, grateful to Don Taylor (McGill University) and Rom Harré (Oxford and Georgetown Universities) for their continued friendship, tall tales, and imaginative advice.

It has been a special pleasure to work with Debbie Carvalko, who skillfully launched this project at Praeger.

CHAPTER 1

Why Consider the Terrorists' Point of View?

"Crazy!" "Immoral!" "Suicidal!" These are the kinds of reactions we instinctively show when confronted by terrorist acts. Terrorists appear to be insane, because they kill, destroy, and injure for motives that seem utterly incomprehensible to the rest of us. Surely only mad men would fly planes filled with passengers into occupied buildings, resulting in thousands of deaths and immeasurable financial damage. From our point of view, no sane person would commit such terrifying, destructive acts.

Even if terrorists are capable of logical thought and can put their plans into effect efficiently, they certainly do not have morality, so it seems to us. How can any moral person kill innocent children, women, and men? We have come to see terrorists as morally "disengaged," as having separated from the morality shared by normal human beings.

Clearly, terrorists are suicidal. Their actions reveal they give no value to human life, not even their own lives. They do not seem to care at all if they live or die. How can people who value their own lives be willing to blow themselves up?

THE NEED TO PROGRESS BEYOND IMMEDIATE REACTIONS

These have been our immediate reactions to terrorism, and we feel very strongly that they are justified. After all, civilians like us have been the victims of terrorism all over the world. Sitting in buses and trains on our way to work, relaxing in side-street cafes, shopping in city centers, strolling along sunny streets, waving goodbye to our loved ones at airports, sleeping in our homes, working in our offices—in the midst of these kinds of routine activities we have been the innocent victims of murderous terrorist attacks in our everyday lives. It makes sense for us to see terrorists as "crazy," "immoral," and "suicidal." This is our point of view, arrived at through harsh experience.

Unfortunately our gut reaction to terrorism, justified though it is, does not help us to understand why terrorism takes place or inform us about how to stop it, because this gut reaction severely limits our worldview. In order to better understand terrorism, we also need to see the world from the terrorists' point of view.

But is it really useful to view the world from the terrorists' point of view? Why should we even make the effort? After all, they are the ones harming us. What good is it to adopt their viewpoint? Does that not work in their favor?

In response to these legitimate questions, I would first point out that we do not need to agree with the terrorists' point of view in order to understand it. We must maintain our complete and utter opposition to terrorism, yet try to better understand why terrorists behave the way they do.

Indeed, by coming to an accurate understanding of the terrorists' point of view, we take an important and necessary step toward ending terrorism. Without this accurate understanding, the billions of dollars and hundreds of thousands of people dedicated to the "war on terror" will be wasted. We will continue to enjoy victories in skirmish after skirmish, without ever tasting real success in the war against terrorism, in the Middle East and elsewhere.

From the terrorists' point of view, terrorism is a rational problem-solving strategy.

From the terrorists' point of view, terrorists are sane, moral, and as much in love with life as anyone else. They are not suicidal and they do not see their lives as wasted when they blow themselves up as part of their larger military-political strategy.

From the terrorists' point of view, it is the rest of the world that is immoral and in need of reform, not the terrorist group.

From the terrorists' point of view, on September 11, 2001, the Twin Towers in New York City were attacked in daring commando raids.

From the terrorists' point of view, commandos have been attacking the United States and its forces at home and abroad in a declared world war. Perhaps the American public was not aware of this declared and ongoing world war, but that is because they were not told early enough by the U.S. government.

From the terrorists' point of view, whether the American public did or did not know about the war does not change the nature of the "commando raids" on September 11, 2001.

From the terrorists' point of view, suicide bombers are precision-guided missiles, the only ones that can be afforded by a desperate and materially poor army.

From the terrorists' point of view, the ends justify the means; the ideal society that is the goal of Islamic *Jihadists* justifies everything and anything.

From the terrorists' point of view, organizations labeled as "terrorist" by the U.S. government and its allies are actually social and political organizations often involved in wide-ranging cultural, welfare, and educational programs. Governments around the world have labeled certain groups as "terrorist organizations" and propagated the message that these organizations are only involved in carrying out terrorist acts. For example, groups such as Hamas, the Tamil Tigers, the IRA, the ETA, and the Al Qaeda have been depicted by governments as only concerned with killing innocent civilians, destroying people and property, and creating chaos in societies.

But from the terrorists' point of view, the work of these so-called "terrorist organizations" is also about education, social work, and charity. Most of these groups are well known in their home societies for their tradition of helping the poor, taking care of widows, and providing a safety net for the disadvantaged.

From the terrorists' point of view, Hamas and other such "terrorist" organizations are filling in and doing the work that corrupt local or regional governments are unable or unwilling to do. For example, in the West Bank, Hamas has been able to win support among the local population, particularly among the poorest sector of society, because it serves as an unofficial charity and social work system (this explains the popularity of Hamas, as reflected in their success in elections). Similarly, in Northern Ireland the IRA has served as an unofficial support system for Catholic families, stepping in to help when the local government officials would not or could not. Likewise, the supporters of the Tamil Tigers contend that this organization is in important ways involved in providing education, health, and welfare services; it is not just concerned to carry out "acts of terror," as the Sri Lankan government would claim.

Hezbollah is the classic example of a group depicted in the Western media as only having a "terrorist" function, but seen by many local people in areas such as Lebanon as having a much broader social services function. Hezbollah literally means "party of God," and the group has not only taken on social services functions, but also transformed itself into a political party that participates in democratic elections (the Tamil Tigers, the political wing of the IRA, Hamas, and many other "terrorist" groups also have made or are making this transition). Hezbollah has been effective in setting up schools and clinics, helping needy families, as well as policing and keeping social order in certain regions of Lebanon.

From the terrorists' point of view, organizations such as Hamas, ETA, the Tamil Tigers, the IRA, and Al Qaeda are the true representatives of the interests of downtrodden people, particularly in third world societies. The activities and concerns of these groups are broad and humanitarian, but they also involve attacking "the enemy"—the corrupt local "puppet" governments and the world powers, particularly the United States, who support them. Thus, we can see that from the terrorists' point of view, even the nature and goals of "terrorist organizations" are not as we in the West typically see them.

Irrationality

"Why do these terrorists attack innocent civilians? What do they hope to achieve? They are so irrational!"

The stereotype of terrorists widely held in the West is that they are irrational, and that their strategies are not logically thought out. Again and again, terrorists are discussed as if they are incapable of rational thinking, and their plans are insane.

Since the tragedy of September 11, in particular, irrationality has been ascribed to Al Qaeda. The image popularized of Al Qaeda members in the media is that of a mindless group of zombies, blindly carrying out suicidal attacks that make no sense. Logic and rationality seem to have been swept aside, if they were ever present among Al Qaeda members. But it is instructive to look at this from an alternative perspective.

From the terrorists' point of view, Al Qaeda is implementing a rational strategic plan to achieve its publicly stated goals. Most of the Western public remains unaware of these goals, because the horrific acts carried out by terrorists capture the headlines and their stated strategic objectives remain buried in the footnotes of any discussion. It is difficult to focus on the strategic objectives of terrorists when one is reading stories about the gruesome results of yet another terrorist bombing.

But these goals are not very difficult to fathom out. They are reflected in various public declarations, and particularly in the statements made by Bin Laden and other Al Qaeda leaders. In summary, these goals are to

1. drive both overt and covert U.S. forces out of Muslim lands in the Near and Middle East (covert American forces have not left Saudi Arabia, the country that houses the most important Islamic

holy places, including Mecca, the prime destination for millions of Muslim pilgrims from around the world each year);
2. stop the unqualified U.S. military and political support for Israel;
3. end the U.S. support for, and manipulation of, corrupt puppet regimes in Saudi Arabia and other dictatorships of the Near East, Middle East, and North Africa.

Toward achieving these goals, from the terrorists' point of view Al Qaeda has tried to compensate for the huge disparity between its forces and that of the United States by expanding the range of strategies it employs. Obviously Al Qaeda cannot fight the U.S. military head-on, because to do so would be to commit organizational suicide. A more rational fighting strategy, from the terrorists' point of view, is to try to influence U.S. decision making through the electorate.

From the terrorists' point of view, the U.S. population elects the U.S. president (albeit indirectly) and the representatives and senators who make important political decisions. Consequently, the U.S. population has some responsibility for what Al Qaeda sees as U.S. military attacks against Muslim nations, and thus the U.S. population is seen as a legitimate military target in the war between Al Qaeda and the United States. By attacking civilian populations in the United States, the United Kingdom, and other "occupying" countries, from the terrorists' point of view it will be possible to influence elections and policies.

From the terrorists' point of view, the rational nature of this approach is demonstrated by what took place in the Spanish elections of March 2004. The Spanish government led by Prime Minister Jose Maria Aznar had stood firmly with the United States as an ally in the invasion of Iraq in 2003. There was some popular support for the withdrawal of Spanish troops from Iraq, but the government ignored these calls. Mariano Rajoy, the ruling party candidate to replace Mr. Aznar, promised to continue the same policies and maintain Spanish troops in Iraq. On March 11, 2004, immediately before the Spanish general elections, a series of bomb explosions on trains in Madrid resulted in close to 200 deaths and over 1,000 serious injuries. After initially blaming ETA, Basque separatists, the government was forced to admit that Al Qaeda was responsible for the deadly attacks. The Spanish voters reacted by voting out the ruling party, and the incoming Spanish government withdrew Spanish troops from Iraq.

From the terrorists' point of view, the withdrawal of Spanish troops from Iraq was the result of a rational war strategy that included attacks on civilians.

Al Qaeda-inspired terrorist attacks have been designed to achieve maximum impact using minimum resources—the biggest "bang for the buck." For example, on July 7, 2005, just at the start of the G-8 Summit hosted by Prime Minister Tony Blair in Edinburgh, Scotland, four bomb explosions brought the London public transportation system to a halt and the entire business and social life of the city to a standstill. The world media was already in Edinburgh to cover the meeting of leaders from the most important industrialized countries, but suddenly Mr. Blair and the world media had to rush south to London and attention was on terrorism, and particularly on Al Qaeda and its claims, supposedly made on behalf of the "true Muslim world." Given the goals of terrorists inspired by Al Qaeda, the July 7 bomb attacks were rational— even though we rightly see these deadly attacks as horrendous and criminal.

Similarly, the extension of terrorist activities to Jordan is part of the larger rational terrorist strategy. The opening up of a war front in Iraq has given Islamic terrorists an opportunity to use Iraq as a staging post to recruit and to launch attacks against what they see to be vulnerable pro-American regimes in the region. On November 9, 2005, bombs almost simultaneously ripped through three "Western" hotels, the Grand Hyatt Hotel, the Radisson SAS Hotel, and the Days Inn Hotel in Amman, killing fifty-four and seriously wounding hundreds, including Americans.

As a result of this vicious attack, the U.S.-backed King of Jordan has been forced to further strengthen his security forces and to crack down even harsher on political and civil activities. Consequently, the lack of freedom and democracy in Jordan is further highlighted, leaving the monarchy more vulnerable to criticism, both at home and abroad. The United States is left in the uncomfortable situation of preaching democracy, but supporting monarchy in Jordan (as well as in Saudi Arabia and some other states). Thus, from the terrorists' point of view, violence has a strategic purpose in dealing with regimes such as the monarchy in Jordan.

In order to better predict what Al Qaeda and the new breed of international terrorists will do, we must appreciate that from the terrorists' point of view, first, violence is not the monopoly of state authorities and, second, national boundaries are irrelevant. Thus, terrorists see it as legitimate for them to use violence, including against civilians, to achieve political goals. They refuse to allow "legitimate governments" to enjoy a monopoly over violence, through "legal" national and regional military forces (such as NATO).

Second, the new breed of international terrorist groups, such as Al Qaeda, are very different from the IRA, ETA, and other such "territorially bounded" groups that restricted their activities within certain national boundaries (for example, the IRA within Great Britain and ETA within Spain). There are now no territorial restrictions from the new terrorists' point of view. Twenty-first-century terrorists are global and literally treat the world as a global village.

Peace at Any Price?

"Why are they so violent? Why don't they use peaceful means? Why don't they see that we must have peace, at any price?"

Terrorists are depicted in the Western media, and often in the world media dominated by the West, as violent people, as enemies of peace. The only news reported about groups such as Al Qaeda concerns their murderous attacks. When such attacks are examined in terms of their origins and motives, the conclusions typically depict terrorists as opposing peace. From the point of view of most Western media, terrorists loathe peace, whereas the United States and other Western democracies support peace.

From the terrorists' point of view, there can be no peace without justice—as justice is defined by them of course. This is a vital point, because it is on this issue that terrorists gain some sympathy in parts of the world—both Western and non-Western. Sympathy for espoused terrorist causes is associated with, and may arise from, American foreign policy and related sentiments of anti-Americanism.

As indicated by the findings of the *Pew Global Attitudes Project*, anti-Americanism is on the rise, even in Britain, a traditional ally of the United States. For example, between 2000 and 2004, the favorability rating of the United States went down from 83 percent to 58 percent in Britain, from 62 percent to 37 percent in France, from 52 percent to 30 percent in Turkey, and from 77 percent to 27 percent in Morocco. The mood of anti-Americanism sweeping across much of Western Europe, the Middle East, Latin America, and some other parts of the world is in part grounded on the idea that there is no peace because there is no justice, and the source of a lot of injustice is seen to be U.S. foreign policy.

In the twenty-first century the United States has increased its rhetoric regarding support for democracy, and there is genuine effort on the part of some individuals in the U.S. government to support democratic movements in at least some parts of the world. This is accompanied by a new candor among U.S. representatives on the world stage; Condoleezza Rice, the U.S. Secretary of State, made the following bold declaration during a visit to the Middle East in June 2005: "For 60 years, my country, the United States, pursued stability at the expense of democracy in this region here in the Middle East, and we achieved neither. Now we are taking a different course. We are supporting the democratic aspirations of all people."[1] The United States seems to be ready to turn a new leaf and to support peace alongside justice, rather than peace instead of justice, at least in some parts of the world. This new orientation is not just reflected in speeches, but is being backed by some action: the United States is exerting some influence to try to create at least the image of more openness in Egypt and other dictatorial societies in some parts of the third world.

Later in this book, I will further discuss how dictators in Egypt and other countries of the Near and Middle East are crushing secular opposition groups, so that opposition to their regimes can only rise up from the mosques. This leaves the West with a lose-lose choice: either support the continuation of dictatorships or stand by and witness Islamic fundamentalists gain control of more regions of the Near and Middle East.

Terrorist Reactions and Liberal Reactions to "Democracy in Islamic Societies"

From the terrorists' point of view, there are three points to highlight in reaction to the "exportation of democracy" the United States has embarked on. Underlying these three points is the idea that the United States is not trustworthy; that behind the words of U.S. politicians lies an alternative reality.

1. From the terrorists' point of view, the United States does not really want true democracy in Islamic societies; what it wants is regimes that U.S. agencies can control. Critics point to a long series of democratic movements in different non-Western countries, from Iran in the early 1950s, Egypt in the 1960s, Algeria in the 1980s, Venezuela in the 1990s, and Brazil and Bolivia in the first decade of the new millennium, which have been overtly and/or covertly opposed by the United States and other Western powers, because they threatened U.S. interests.

2. From the terrorists' point of view, this new "pro-democracy" policy of the United States is only designed to control third world societies using a new strategy, one required by the demands of the twenty-first century. From the terrorists' point of view, the United States and other Western powers only seem interested to support democracies when they result in pro-Western governments.

   The United States has learned that democracy in the Third World is like a tiger, and riding a tiger can be very dangerous and unpredictable. Popular movements in the Third World have brought to power the likes of Khomeini in Iran and Chavez in Venezuela—populist leaders who can win elections, but at the same time are strongly anti-American. The United States does its best to topple these kinds of 'democracies.'

3. Most importantly, from the point of view of certain groups of terrorists, including most of those inspired by fundamentalist interpretations of Islam, democracy is an undesirable goal because it does not fit in with their vision of an ideal world.

From the point of view of these terrorists, democracy gives too much freedom to humans to choose to go down new paths and to create new types of social relationships and new types of social and political structures. Such choices, such freedoms, can easily lead people away from an ideal Islamic society as the fundamentalists see it.

Of course, at home and abroad critics of U.S. foreign policy tend to endorse points (1) and (2) above. That is, critics suspect that, first, the United States continues to oppose true democracy. For example, they point out that even in postwar Iraq, under the eyes of the world media, the United States has tried to intervene in elections and to manipulate the "free" Iraqi media, in favor of certain candidates, such as the American-funded acting Prime Minister Iyad Alawi (who later turned against U.S. policies in Iraq, at least in public). Second, critics tend to suspect that the United States is using its influence to try to overthrow left-wing leaders who come to power, even when they are democratically elected in Venezuela, Brazil, and elsewhere.

But on the global stage, agreement on points (1) and (2) above is not limited to liberal and intellectual critics of U.S. foreign policy. The enormous rise in anti-Americanism among ordinary people around the world, including in Western Europe, is associated with the feeling many people have that the American government is only supportive of democracy in the Third World when the elected Third World governments have pro-U.S. policies and favor American business interests. This perception has meant that support for the United States in the "war on terror" is not as strong as it should be, even in Western Europe and even to the point of arguing that the term terrorist is meaningless because "one person's terrorist is another person's freedom fighter."

The "One Person's Freedom Fighter . . . " Argument

In this discussion, I use the term terrorism to mean *politically motivated violence, perpetrated by individuals, groups, or state-sponsored agents, intended to bring about feelings of terror and helplessness in a civilian population in order to influence decision making and to change behavior.* I do not accept the view that "the term terrorist is meaningless because one person's terrorist is another person's freedom fighter." However, I do accept that the actions of a number of governments, including that of the United States and other Western governments, has made it seem legitimate to argue that "one person's freedom fighter is another person's terrorist."

Within the U.S. government there are a variety of different entities, some more pro-democracy than others, both in their goals and methods. Certain entities have supported terrorist activities against governments unfriendly to the United States. Consider, for example, the willingness of the U.S. government to support the likes of Luis Posada Carriles, a Cuban exile and an anti-Castro activist who according to international standards qualifies as a terrorist, but has also been hailed as a "freedom fighter" by anti-Castro forces. Mr. Carriles worked for the CIA from 1961 to 1967 and in February 2005 he somehow reentered the United States, seeking political asylum in an effort to escape prosecution for committing terrorist acts, including killing an Italian visitor in an attack on tourist spots in Havana in 1997. Evidence also implicates Mr. Carriles in the bombing of a Cuban commercial airliner that killed seventy-three people in 1976. A similar case is that of Mr. Orlando Bosch, a leading member of a violent anti-Castro group in Florida, seen by anti-Castro groups and some in the U.S. government as a "freedom fighter," but by many international observers as a "terrorist." In 1989 the U.S. Justice Department did indeed call Mr. Bosch a terrorist and moved to deport him. However, a year later the first Bush administration overruled the deportation and Mr. Bosch has been allowed to remain in the United States.[2]

These and other similar cases seem to strengthen the argument that "one person's terrorist is another person's freedom fighter." The danger is that the term "terrorist" will be seen as only a political weapon, so that "our guys" are always freedom fighters and only "their guys" are the terrorists.

Fortunately, most people recognize that bombing a Cuban civilian plane and bombing an American civilian plane are both acts of terrorism, no matter how the different governments label the acts. We may disagree about the details of a definition, but in practice most reasonable people agree that if it walks like a terrorist, shoots like a terrorist, and explodes bombs like a terrorist, then it is a terrorist.

The Power of Context

My goal in this book is to explain the world from the terrorists' point of view, and in so doing reveal how we can bring an end to terrorism. My focus is on how certain social conditions give rise to a morality supportive of terrorism. The power of such contexts is so great, and the pressures on individuals to obey and to conform so crushing, that many choose to endorse a morality supportive of terrorism, and some go further and carry out acts of terrorism on the basis of this morality.

Although individuals always have some measure of free will to choose the path of action they will take, in some conditions the situational factors make one path far more likely than other paths. There are numerous ways in which the power of context shows itself in our everyday lives and leads us to make everyday decisions in particular ways. For example, although John could choose to wear a bright red and yellow tie at his uncle's funeral in New York, he is very likely to choose a dark, somber tie instead; just as when John gets married, his future wife could choose to follow an alternative fashion trend and wear a black dress at their wedding, but she is far more likely to wear a white dress. In each case, the individual choices, John deciding to wear a dark tie at a funeral and his bride deciding to wear a white dress at their wedding, are made with some measure of free will and we can hold the individuals responsible for their choices, but we must also accept that their choices were heavily influenced by the social contexts (of a funeral and a wedding).

My contention is that terrorism is explained by the power of context. Although we can and must hold individual terrorists personally responsible for their actions, the most effective way to root out terrorism is to change the contexts that give rise to a morality supporting terrorism.

CHAPTER 2

Identity Needs and Globalization

IDENTITY PARADOXES IN THE GLOBAL VILLAGE

There were four of us in the cramped, noise-filled cabin of the military helicopter: a bureaucrat from the United Nations headquarters in New York, a young woman journalist wearing an Islamic *chador* that most of the time covered her body and head and only left her eyes and hands exposed to the world, a flirtatious and handsome young male pilot who was imitating characters from *Top Gun*, and me. We could see three other helicopters leading the way up ahead, hugging the hills to escape Iraqi artillery fire. It was 1982 and I was accompanying a United Nations "fact finding" mission to the Iran–Iraq war front. The imminent danger was that we would be shot out of the sky. Some other dangers facing the mission were more bizarre. For example, just that morning we had woken up to discover that overnight a large U.S. flag had been painted on the ground at the entrance to our sleeping quarters, so that anyone entering or leaving the building would symbolically trample on the "Great Satan."

The helicopter pilot talked mostly with the charming female journalist, but everyone was huddled so close together that the rest of us could not help overhearing. The young pilot planned to move to California, to join his uncle and to help him operate a string of dry-cleaning stores.

"My uncle doesn't have children, so he needs my help. I know America, I was in Texas for my pilot training," he explained proudly.

"Did you buy your boots in Texas?" she asked. Clint Eastwood might have worn those gnarled Texas boots in one of his spaghetti Western movies.

The pilot grinned and nodded. "I'm going back soon, my uncle knows a lawyer who can help me get a visa."

At every step of this war mission "Death to America!" had been shouted at us by countless Iranians, by government officials, by chanting crowds, and by endless slogans on walls. The helicopter we were in had "Death to America" slogans written on it. Yet every day brought us face to face with Iranians from all walks of life who asked for help to get visas to the United States.

"Such a paradox," said the man from the U.N. headquarters, shaking his head, "Such a paradoxical people. One minute they shout death to America, the next minute they ask me for help to get them a visa to America."

Anyone who wants to understand the roots of terrorism has to come to grips with the simultaneous attraction and repulsion, love and hate, that Islamic societies experience toward the United States. On the one hand, people in Islamic societies, even fundamentalist Muslims, are strongly attracted to the United States, and many would jump at the opportunity to immigrate to America. On the other hand, the same people often have very negative feelings, and even intense hatred, toward the United States.

The situation in Iran reflects a general ambivalence of Muslim communities around the world toward the West in general and the United States in particular. The West represents technological advancement, and for many people, particularly some groups of women and minorities, the West represents freedom and liberation from stifling traditions. On the other hand, the West represents an alternative identity into which non-Westerners can merge, disappear, and lose all traces of authenticity. The anguish of losing authentic identity, of disappearing into the identity of the other, is felt by the North African youth rioting in France, the Lebanese youth rioting in Australia, as it is felt by the Palestinian youth rioting in the West Bank, as it is felt by the youth shouting "Death to America" in Tehran.

At the heart of Islamic terrorism is the crisis of identity in Islamic communities. But we cannot comprehend this crisis from the traditional view of Western researchers, who tend to see identity as something static, stable, and based on so-called "universal traits," such as openness to experience, conscientiousness, extroversion, agreeableness, and neuroticism (the so-called "big-five" personality traits). Rather than objective, such a trait-based view of identity is highly limited to a particular time in a particular part of Western culture. An alternative, more useful approach is to view identity as dynamic and in flux through persons evolving in and with their cultural context.

Individuals incorporate and assimilate into their identities those aspects of the world that make their lives more meaningful and fulfilled. People continually change themselves, as they shed and take on, subtract and add, reconstruct and reevaluate different aspects of identity. They do not simply "show anger," "feel shame," and "demonstrate aggression," but they become angry, shamed, and aggressive persons. They come to see themselves as a person who is angry, is shamed, and is aggressive. Their view of the sort of persons they are, and not just what they do, changes continually.

Some individuals become terrorists, taking on the morality of terrorism as part of their personal identity. Becoming a terrorist is more than just taking part in terrorist activities; it is transforming the self to arrive at a particular identity. The nature of this identity derives from the crisis being experienced by Islamic communities. We can understand this better by first reviewing different alternative explanations of terrorism.

THE SEARCH FOR EXPLANATIONS OF TERRORISM: LESSONS FROM THE MAJOR THEORIES

Those who seek out social science theories to explain terrorism will not be disappointed in the number of theories available, although they may be disappointed in the explanatory power of each theory independent of other theories.[3] In many respects, the available theories tend to complement rather than to compete with one another. We can still benefit from the major theories, by considering their collective insights and arriving at a broad explanation based on received wisdom. However, we also need to progress beyond currently available explanations, and that is where a focus on identity becomes essential.

The major theories adopt a wide range of perspectives on humankind, from those that view humans as irrational and unable to correctly recognize both what their actions are and what lies behind their actions, to those that see humans as rational and guided by material interests. The irrationalist perspective is deeply influenced by the writings of Sigmund Freud (1856–1939), and in modern research it is best represented by Terror Management Theory. Irrationality also characterizes a number of other theories that have justice as their central theme, the most important example of this category being Relative Deprivation Theory and the Just World Theory. To some degree, irrationality is also a feature of functional, evolutionary-based theories. Finally, a number of materialist theories assume that humans are rational and self-centered, and that they strive to maximize their personal profits (defined in a variety of different ways).

The Freudian Legacy: Humans as Irrational

Although the unconscious was discussed by various writers before Freud, it was Freud's writings that placed the unconscious at the center of scientific and artistic depictions of human thought and action. After Freud, it became the norm for not only writers and researchers, but also ordinary people in their everyday lives, to wonder about unconscious motives and thoughts that might lie behind actions, particularly the actions of others rather than ourselves. Freud's writings on aggression and war have proved to be highly insightful, because they cast light on important aspects of human behavior that seem out of control and out of the bounds of rationality.

Humans have repeatedly engulfed themselves in "wars to end all wars," and "wars to spread liberty and freedom," and yet each additional war seems to bring nothing but more death and destruction. Our newest rational "fig leaf" is the idea that democracies do not wage war against one another, so if we wage war and convert all countries to democracy, we will put an end to war. But this fig leaf cannot hide the fact that Hitler was elected to power, and then set off the events leading to World War Two with mass popular support (of course, critics would contend that the elections that Hitler "won" were flawed, but the same could be said of some other Western elections, such as the U.S. presidential elections in 2000). A variety of modern dictators, including Khomeini who led Iran in an eight-year-long bloody war against Iraq, have enjoyed mass popular support and would win "democratic" elections.

No matter how we dress up human actions, war and aggression seem to be difficult if not impossible to explain by assuming humans to be rational agents. In this domain of behavior, at least, it is more plausible that humans really remain largely unaware of, and unable to control, the forces that influence them.

Surely there is nothing more irrational than suicide bombers blowing themselves up, killing and injuring innocent civilians? Terrorism seems to be a type of behavior that is ideally suited to assessment through Freud's ideas.

Freud gave the highest importance to group life, and the influence of groups on individual members. This influence comes about primarily through the identification of group members with the group leader; Freud argued that the only groups capable of effective and organized action are groups with strong leaders. It is through the leader, such as Jesus Christ for the Catholic Church or the Commander in Chief for an army, that group members are emotionally bound together.

The leader serves to tie all the group members together in love, just as family members are emotionally bound together. The head of the church and the head of the army serve as substitute fathers, just as Osama bin Laden serves as a substitute father for Al Qaeda. The leader guides members to love one another as brothers and sisters within the group, and this "illusion of mutual love" serves as the basis for group solidarity and cohesion.

But in Freudian psychology emotional ties always have a negative as well as a positive side, reflecting destructive as well as constructive forces in human nature. In all love relationships, there is hatred and enmity, both manifest and latent. Love and hate always exist side by side. Even between two lovers who pine and suffer when they are apart, there are also negative emotions. That is how the same lovers who today sigh for one another and are in anguish when they are apart, can sometimes end up fighting ferociously and dragging one another screaming through divorce courts.

In order to survive and function effectively, groups need mechanisms for coping with the negative emotions that build up inside the group. Freud demonstrates his genius by identifying the mechanism of displacement, which allows the group leader to redirect negative sentiments to a target outside the group. Thus, group members get to love one another, and to redirect their negative, destructive feelings onto outsiders.

The more dissimilar an out-group is, the more likely it is to be selected as a target for displaced aggression. From a Freudian perspective, the targeting of ethnic minorities in hate crimes and discrimination generally, is just one manifestation of displaced aggression. Those who are seen to be different, "outsiders," become natural targets of individuals who show love for one another within their own group.

The Freudian message is clear: We can all love one another, as long as there are some people left over to hate as outsiders. From this perspective, Islamic fundamentalists can bind together their people in love, as long as the "Great Satan" represented by the United States is there to hate. Similarly, from this perspective after the cold war and the collapse of the Soviet empire, the United States needed another external enemy to use as the target of displaced aggression, and Islamic fundamentalism was constructed as the new "barbarian enemy at our gates."

Terror Management

Twenty-first century researchers have given the irrational model a new twist, in the shape of Terror Management Theory.[4] This theory begins with the mundane observation that like all other organisms humans are motivated to preserve their own lives. A second observation is that humans are self-aware: we recognize that one day all of us will die. Out of these two obvious points comes a startling claim: the combined outcome of self-awareness and the self-preservation motive is a potential for experiencing overwhelming terror.

How do we prevent ourselves from becoming immobilized by feelings of terror? According to the theory, we cope by constructing cultures with worldviews that serve to protect us from feelings of terror, and allow us to function effectively despite the inevitability of death. These worldviews are holistic, in that they include religious values and beliefs about how the world began, how it will end, and how our lives will continue even after we die and leave our present world. By giving meaning to life and conceiving death as just a passage to another, everlasting life, we avoid the feelings of despair, meaninglessness, and terror that can make life seem utterly pointless.

> Life's but a walking shadow, a poor player
> That struts and frets his hour upon the stage
> And then is heard no more. It is a tale
> Told by an idiot, full of sound and fury
> Signifying nothing.
> *Macbeth* (Act V, scene v, lines 24–28)

Despite the death-denying role of our cultures, the inevitability of mortality means that we are continuously confronted by the challenge of coping with the thought and reality of death. This challenge becomes particularly acute when we, often unintentionally, come across worldviews that are very different from our own. For example, if it is a central part of my belief system that those of my faith will all go directly to heaven and those of your faith will go to hell, and you believe that those of my faith will go directly to hell and only those of your faith will go to heaven, according to our belief systems one of us is utterly mistaken. Our encounters can only serve to remind us of our mortality, and lead us to feel anxiety about our ultimate fate.

In addition to adopting death-protective cultural worldviews, we deal with anxiety arising from the certainty of death and the constant reminders of mortality through a range of mechanisms, from conversion to annihilation. At the benign end of this range of strategies, a person might *convert* to another worldview. For example, I might become convinced that your faith has the correct account of how one gets to heaven, and convert so as to try to get to heaven along your path. However, conversion is rarely done voluntarily. An alternative is for your group to abandon your faith and *assimilate* into mine, or alternatively to adopt *accommodation*, by simply taking on those aspects of my faith that are more to your liking. Another, more sinister possibility that has occurred to various killers over the ages is that your group may decide to try to annihilate my group, resulting in the total destruction of a group (as has happened throughout human existence, and in recent history through colonization).

Supporters claim that the terror management theory is validated by evidence showing that self-esteem serves to buffer anxiety: Our culture allows us to lead meaningful lives, enjoy high self-esteem, and thus avoid mortality-induced anxiety. Obviously for many people a central, and often the most important, component of a cultural worldview is framed by religious beliefs. Religion acts as the "opium of the people," to borrow a Marxist phrase, in the sense that it relieves anxiety about mortality.

Joe is a Christian fundamentalist and believes strongly that he enjoys a special place in the sight of God, and Ahmed is an Islamic fundamentalist who also believes strongly in his special place in the sight of God. Terror Management Theory suggests that both Joe and Ahmed enjoy high self-esteem and are protected from mortality-induced anxiety by their religious belief systems. This is an insightful idea, and can help explain some forms of ethnocentrism and discrimination against out-groups: obviously Joe and Ahmed will tend to view the out-group as wrong and even evil.

However, how good an explanation is this of suicide terrorists? Do unconscious motives associated with an overwhelming terror of death drive suicide terrorists to blow up both themselves and others? My view is that this explanation is far-fetched and misses the mark, because suicide terrorists show by their actions that they are not seriously afraid of death. However, there are aspects of Terror Management Theory that are worth considering as part of a wider explanation of Islamic terrorism.

In particular, Terror Management Theory has correctly identified the terrifying threat posed by those who challenge the worldview of "true believers." I do not accept this is because such external threats remind us of our mortality, but believe it is because they question the value of something that is essential to us here and now: our authentic identity, both personal and collective.

The Complex Being: Humans as Both Rational and Irrational

Freud and modern adherents to the irrationalist model present a view of human thought and action that is too extreme, depicting too large a role for irrationality and the unconscious. But there are a number of different alternative theories that view humans as a mixture of rationality and irrationality. The "irrationality" in these theories still arises from the assumption that humans are not aware of what really influences their thoughts and actions, but a large role is also given to the rational aspects of human life.

An example of this "mixed" perspective is *sociobiology*, the scientific study of the biological basis of behavior. Sociobiologists highlight the adaptive functions of aggression in the long-term survival of humans in changing environmental conditions. The *selfish gene* thesis proposed by Richard Dawkins suggests that the real competition for survival in evolution is between gene pools and that we humans serve as convenient carriers of genes.[5] We are influenced by a "whispering within" to cooperate with and be altruistic toward others who are more genetically similar to us, but to be aggressive and hostile against those who are genetically dissimilar to us.

Consider, for example, a situation in which you had to sacrifice yourself for another person. There are five of you stranded on a sinking ship, and there is only space for one more person in the last lifeboat. Who will you want to place in the lifeboat: yourself, your aunt, a good friend, a very interesting man you met on the ship, a friend of your son's, or your son? Most people do not hesitate to say they would want to place their son, their own "flesh and blood," in the lifeboat. Why is this? Sociobiologists would argue it is because your son carries your genes and can pass on your genes to another generation.

But what if you have two sons in the ship with you, one adopted and the other your "natural" offspring?

Sociobiologists would predict that you would give preference to your natural offspring, and there is strong evidence in support of this claim. In general, there is more likelihood of parents sacrificing for their natural offspring than for adopted children, and there is more likelihood of adopted children getting injured or killed at home than natural offspring.[6] At the interpersonal level, then, the sociobiological thesis receives a lot of support. But at the larger intergroup level, sociobiological accounts are far less convincing.

A major shortcoming of the sociobiological account at the intergroup level is the invalid assumption that people can use phenotype, "looks," to accurately determine genotype, "genetic characteristics." Second, it is assumed that people will use this inferred knowledge to show more positive behavior toward genetically more similar others. But this prediction is not supported by patterns of coalitions in major wars. For example, during both the first and the second World Wars, England was supported by colonies such as India to fight against Germany and its allies, which included the Japanese; this is not a pattern compatible with sociobiology. Surely the English should have been allied with the Germans to fight against "dissimilar" others such as the Japanese and the Indians?

How does sociobiology fare in explaining terrorism? The outcome is mixed. On the one hand, it could be claimed that the September 11 terrorists were attacking what they (unconsciously) saw as carriers of competing genes. Similarly, Islamic fundamentalist attacks in Western population centers, most famously Madrid and London, could be interpreted as attempts to annihilate or weaken genetic competitors.

On the other hand, suicide bombings in Iraq and much of the Islamic world have for the most part resulted in the deaths of other Muslims. For example, the November 2005 hotel bombings in Aman, Jordan, killed fifty-eight people, the vast majority of them Jordanians (only two of the dead were Americans). In Iraq, my estimate is that terrorist attacks have killed about twenty-five Iraqis for every one American.

Justice Theories

But if sociobiologists have a mixed success in explaining terrorist attacks, the justice theories have an even more difficult time. The main reason is that the influential justice theories were developed in the context of Western societies, where the main research puzzle has been: why do people put up with injustice and continue to interpret the world as just, even in situations when it obviously is not just? Related to this question is the puzzle of inaction: why do people remain passive in the face of enormous injustices? Why do people not do anything to try to change the world toward what they think would be more fair?

These are appropriate and legitimate questions in contexts where enormous inequalities and injustices persist and where in many cases the kind of justice people receive depends on the legal advice they can afford, yet there is general acceptance of the status quo.

In the Western context, Mel Lerner's proposition that people are motivated to see the world as just makes a lot of sense.[7] By blaming the victim ("It was her own fault she was sexually assaulted; she shouldn't have been wearing that low-cut dress in a bar") by shifting our focus from the short-term to the long-term ("Oh, everything evens out and becomes fair in the end") and other similar strategies, we are able to maintain a view of the world as fair and thus avoid having to take action to change the situation.

Similarly, System Justification Theory[8] is very appropriate for addressing the question: why do people continue to endorse a social system that perpetuates inequalities and unfairness? Why do they remain passive? One answer, inspired by Marx, is that the rich control the media, the education system, the established churches, and all the other means through which we are taught to see the world. The rich use this influence to ensure that we see the world as fair, and we interpret events in ways that justifies the existing social system. Because we are not fully aware of this process, we are to some extent at least irrational.

But terrorists are not passive and they do not see the world as just. Terrorists view the world as unjust and take the most atrocious, extremist actions to try to change the world toward what they think is ideal. Explanations such as the "Just World Theory" and "System Justification

Theory" do not do a good job of explaining terrorism, although they are very useful in most contexts, both Western and non-Western.

Relative Deprivation

When I compare my income to that of Bill Gates, I feel relatively deprived; but when I compare my income to that of most graduate students, I feel well off. This is *egoistical* or personal deprivation. We all intuitively know about the relationship between comparison target and feelings of egoistical deprivation, and we routinely use this knowledge to manipulate how we feel and how others feel. For example, if I want to get a graduate student to feel less deprived, I might urge her to compare herself to other graduate students who are working with far less resources. A neighbor who has a leaky roof is consoled with the words, "It could be a lot worse; think of the flood victims in New Orleans."

In some situations, people experience *fraternal deprivation*, relative deprivation because of their groups' positions in society. For example, a Muslim might feel deprived because of the position of Muslims vis-à-vis other groups. Research shows that people who feel fraternal deprivation, and those who experience the double whammy of personal and fraternal deprivation together, are more likely to take part in collective action to try to change their situation.

An even more intriguing proposition from the relative deprivation literature is that rebellion and revolution is more likely to happen at times of rising prosperity. As people become better off, a danger is that their expectations rise faster and faster. If my rising expectations are not met, then I feel deprivation—comparing my situation with where I think I should be. If I used to have a bicycle and now have a motorbike, I will still feel deprived if I believe I should have two cars by now.

Rapidly rising expectations undoubtedly played a role in the run up to the 1978–1979 revolution in Iran. The rapid rise in oil prices and unwise, lofty claims by the Shah raised expectations among Iranians: Iran was to become the Switzerland of the East. Despite rapid economic change and improvements in the standard of living for many if not most Iranians, there was no way in which the rapidly rising expectations of the Iranian population could be met.

Ayatollah Khomeini managed the situation very differently. Following a pattern familiar in all revolutions, before coming to power Khomeini focused on the rights of the people to various freedoms, but after the revolution he shifted his emphasis to the duties of the people to obey authorities.[9] This shift helped to lower expectations about freedoms. At the same time, Khomeini emphatically declared that the revolution had not been for material benefits, it had been for Islam. The material rewards of this world do not matter; it is only the next world that matters. Thus, Khomeini dramatically lowered the expectations of Iranians for improvements in their standard of living.

But at the same time, Khomeini made the common people *feel involved* in the government and the procedures of decision making. After a nationwide referendum on whether or not Iran should be declared an Islamic Republic in early 1979, there were numerous elections at national, regional, and local levels. It did not much matter that the elections could only have one outcome, because only vetted so-called "Islamic" candidates could participate. The essential point is that, particularly at the local level, people felt they were participants in the procedures of justice and decision making.

From the viewpoint of Relative Deprivation Theory, terrorism is an outcome of rising, unmet expectations, and increasing frustration among millions of young people who feel they have no voice, no hope, and no possibilities for a brighter future as things stand. The expectations of these young people have been raised in part by globalization—improved communications make available images and voices of other worlds, where young people have much better possibilities to develop their talents and live a fulfilled life. The young in Islamic societies see how life could be—the rich educational opportunities, the consumer goods, and social and political freedoms—but in their own societies they see no opportunities to achieve such a life.

Most importantly, the international media has changed how young people in Islamic communities think about their own identities and respond to basic questions about themselves: What sort of person am I? How am I seen and valued by others? The answers to these questions depend in large part on how they think their group is seen. In many Islamic communities, in both Western and non-Western societies, the young have come to see themselves as belonging to a deprived, unfairly treated group. This image of the self and the ingroup as unfairly treated, as downtrodden, has profound consequences, and I return to this topic later in this discussion.

Materialist Explanations

At the other extreme from Freud's psychodynamic, irrationalist theory are a set of materialist theories that for the most part assume human behavior to be rational. The goal of human beings, according to the materialist theories, is to maximize their own pleasure (through maximizing profits, for example). This goal is pursued through decision-making that, albeit sometimes biased and/or mistaken, is nevertheless for the most part conscious and rational.

The materialist theories assume that human consciousness and psychological experience is shaped by materialist conditions. Consider an example in the area of conflict: nation X and nation Y both want oil, competition for oil leads to intergroup hostilities and the two nations end up hating one another. Thus, the (negative) feelings and (aggressive) actions the nations have toward each other are shaped by their competition for oil. Negative feelings and actions would end if one or both nations decide they do not want oil, for example because they have discovered alternative sources of energy.

An intriguing version of materialist theory is Resource Mobilization Theory,[10] which proposes that group discontent and collective movements can be shaped by those who control resources. From this viewpoint, collective movements are not initiated by psychological feelings of injustice and discontent, because through the control of resources it is possible to manufacture psychological feelings of injustice and discontent.

Consider, for example, the case of the women's movement that helped to bring about the civil rights legislation of the late 1960s in the United States. Why did women not mobilize in earlier historical eras? Is it because women were materially better off during earlier eras? Did women enjoy greater freedom or more expansive rights in the nineteenth century, the sixteenth century, or the eleventh century? Obviously, women were in a worse situation in earlier centuries.

According to resource mobilization theory, what was different about the post-World War Two era is that the elite who controlled resources recognized that it was now in their interests to improve the education and technical training of women and engage them in the workforce outside the home. Because of this recognition, those who controlled resources helped to mobilize women and launch the women's liberation movement, with the result that it is now the norm for women to work outside the home in Western societies. Thus, feelings of deprivation and the need to take collective action were instigated and shaped by an elite in control of resources.

How effective is the rationalist, materialist perspective in explaining terrorism? Are terrorist groups rational and motivated to maximize profits? On the one hand, it could be argued that Al Qaeda and other terrorist groups are determined to gain control of territory and other material resources, as reflected for example by their efforts to expel Westerners from Islamic lands (such as Saudi Arabia and Iraq). On the other hand, terrorists are often willing to sacrifice their own lives and destroy resources. In Iraq and elsewhere, terrorists seem to be intent on annihilation; their behavior pattern is not compatible with a rational, materialist perspective. A suicide bomber who blows himself up in a crowded public place is not trying to gather material resources through a rational strategy: his only objective is to annihilate the enemy.

A Role for Individual Characteristics?

An alternative theoretical view to explaining terrorism focuses on the characteristics of individual terrorists, and indeed some individual characteristics do play a key role in terrorism. An important characteristic shared by most "foot soldiers" in terrorist groups and organizations is their age, sex, and marital status: most are in their late teens and early twenties, male, and unmarried (despite the much popularized cases of female suicide bombers such as the Belgium-born Muriel Degauque and the Iraqi Sajida al-Rishawi, and increased recruitment of females as suicide bombers; internationally the cases of male suicide bombers outnumber females by about thirty-five males to one female). We should not be surprised by this trend, because terrorism is a form of rebellious, risk-taking behavior, and it is young single males who undertake such behavior in Western societies also.

Consider the tendency for young males to take part in extreme sports in the West. These include roller blading, surfing, games of chicken using tuned-up cars and motorbikes, bungy jumping, and so on. Of course, females and older age groups also engage in extreme sports, but typically it is young men who take the greatest risks. This higher risk taking among males results in higher fatalities among males than females. The birth ratio is about 950 girls to 1,000 males globally, meaning that 5 percent more boys than girls are born. But risk taking results in higher death rates among young males, with the result that the sex ratio evens out among the young adult age group.

Higher testosterone levels among young males is just one biological indicator of physical readiness for higher levels of aggression and risk-taking—a very volatile energy that in most societies is channeled into sports and controlled forms of competition. This becomes particularly clear to anyone who watches teams of young men playing hockey, rugby, football, or other contact sports. The players hurl themselves at one another with ferocious zeal; they love the thrill and excitement associated with risky behavior.

What happens when a high-testosterone young man is channeled into a different, destructive, direction? The result is explosive. We get a glimpse of such situations when rival groups of soccer fans clash in Europe; or when race riots break out in the United States; or when groups of Catholic Irish youth or Protestant Irish youth clash with police in Northern Ireland; or when Palestinian youth fight Israeli security forces. The energy that might have been put into wielding a hockey stick or throwing a ball is now put into clubbing an opponent and hurling stones or bombs.

We must be careful not to exaggerate the association between males and terrorism. Gender roles are in important respects malleable, and there are countless examples of how women can step in and outperform men on tasks that previously had been thought to be the monopoly of males. A constructive example of this is the stupendous success of women in education over the last century. In many parts of the world women are now successfully competing with men in just about every academic field in schools and universities, whereas just a century ago they were excluded from even entering most classrooms. For students of gender roles, it is not at all surprising that because of changed cultural conditions and a more active role for Chechnian, Tamil, and Kurdish–Turk women in their societies generally, significant numbers of terrorist attacks in Chechnia, Sri Lanka, and in Turkey have involved young female terrorists. In a number of bloody attacks, female terrorists have shown that they can match males in risk-taking and aggression.

But elevated risk-taking and aggressivity is only one characteristic of young men and women; another important characteristic is the search for adequate identity. Identity needs serve as a central theme in this book, exploring the terrorists' point of view.

IDENTITY "NEEDS" CREATED BY SOCIAL DEMANDS

Unconscious forces, fear of "the other," feelings of deprivation, perceptions of injustice, a tendency to want to support one's own kin and ethnic group, and the struggle for material resources—these are among the most important factors that play a part in terrorism as suggested by the major theories. But there is an important underlying theme, a "superordinate factor" that explains terrorism far better, and this is to do with identity and the deep and pervasive crisis of identity being experienced by Islamic communities.

A fundamental psychological demand placed on individuals by societies is to achieve an authentic identity, and this social demand creates a "need" in each of us. Throughout our lives, we attempt to satisfy this learned identity need. Three main requirements have to be met in order for authentic identity to be achieved.

1. A prerequisite for authentic identity at the individual level is that authentic identity must first be achieved at the group level; it is not possible for an individual to achieve an authentic personal identity independent from group identity.[11] Individual authenticity arises from collective authenticity; more broadly, individual consciousness arises from collective consciousness.

   At first glance, this claim may seem unacceptable from an American cultural perspective, where "rugged individualism" is celebrated so regularly and loudly. However, consider that the identity associated with "rugged individualism" is itself embedded in, and utterly dependent on, the collective American culture. Characters played by John Wayne and Clint Eastwood, the lone *Shayne*-type cowboy characters who ride into town alone to fight and win the good fight and then ride out of town alone, are actually completely dependent on a particular cultural context. Outside the individualistic ethos of the shared American value system, they lose their authentic identity.

Thus, a first requirement for the development of authentic identity at the level of the individual is that it must first be achieved at the group level. Unfortunately, the identity crisis experienced by Islamic communities means that individual Muslims do not have the collective resources they need in order to achieve authentic identity.

2. A second requirement for an authentic identity is that the main source of identity must be internal to the ingroup (the group to which a person belongs), rather than out-groups (groups to which a person does not belong). The sources of identity include the power sources that determine traditions, values, goals, and other characteristics of the group, including stereotypes (overgeneralizations) about the group.

   Clearly, this requirement for attaining authentic identity is difficult to achieve for many minority groups. This is because in many situations, the main sources of identity for minority groups are majority out-groups. For example, historically the main sources of identity for African Americans and other ethnic minorities have been whites, just as until very recently the main sources of identity for women have been men.

   The main determinant of the sources of identity is group power: groups that enjoy power superiority can shape the identity of groups with less power. Islamic communities do not meet this requirement, because they have suffered from relative weakness vis-à-vis the West. The sources of identity for Islamic communities have been external powers. In particular, the West, through its dominance of the global mass media and entertainment industries, has influenced identity ideals adopted by the younger generation in Islamic communities.

   The West is the main source of the music, films, clothing, books and magazines, video games, electronic communications, and "culture" broadly, which influences youths in Islamic societies. This has created the problem of "imported ideals" and a lack of authenticity in Islamic communities.

3. A third requirement for an authentic identity is distinctiveness; related to which is positiveness. In the Western context, Social Identity Theory has been a highly influential theory arguing that individuals are motivated to achieve a positive and distinct identity

(presumably, this "motivation" is instilled in people through socialization). Thus, individuals want to belong to groups that are both positively evaluated and are perceived to be different in some important respect.

In the Western context, positiveness is viewed as broader and more embracing than distinctiveness. Thus, in the research tradition of Social Identity Theory there has been, often explicitly, a greater emphasis on the proposed need for positive identity than the proposed need for distinctiveness.

But in the global context, minority groups, such as Islamic communities, are confronted by the threat of being overwhelmed by imported cultural systems and identities. True, minority groups are concerned about being evaluated positively, but an even higher priority challenge is for them to retain or manufacture a distinct, different identity. In the global context, distinctiveness has become even more difficult and more essential to achieve than positiveness.

This is because it is possible to gain some measure of positiveness by assimilating into a majority culture, but this would result in complete loss of distinctiveness. For example, Muslim immigrants in France, Australia, and other host countries could abandon their heritage cultures and identities and assimilate into Western culture and gain positive evaluation, but through this strategy they would lose distinctiveness and the characteristics that set them apart. Thus, in some contexts remaining different is a challenge that takes precedence over being evaluated positively, because distinctiveness is a prerequisite for positiveness.

The challenge of achieving authentic identity is made more complex by globalization, particularly for minority groups. Smaller cultural and linguistic groups are under severe pressure to assimilate into larger and larger units.

Of course, globalization does not equate with Westernization. "Becoming global" involves almost countless cross-fertilization processes across different cultures. There are numerous sources of influence other than the United States and Western Europe, an example being India, with its enormously productive film industry. Indian films are now exported to all the different corners of the world, including North America.

Although globalization does not equate with Westernization, globalization does equate with a push toward bigger. That is, in the process of globalization smaller groups often merge into larger ones. This trend, driven by economic factors, runs counter to historical and cultural processes that push to preserve local identities; a complex contradiction that I turn to next.

GLOBAL ECONOMIES, LOCAL IDENTITIES

The juggernaut of globalization is steamrolling over numerous cultural, religious, ethnic, political, and language differences. This economic push is so powerful that it is forcing political giants like Communist China to act against their ideological principles, bend with the winds, adopt a free market economy, and integrate into the world economy. Vietnam is following the same path; despite achieving military victories against representatives of the capitalist world, first France and then the United States, the Vietnamese are being defeated by globalization forces. But the headlong rush toward greater globalization is being blocked by a sentiment that shows up in a variety of ways, such as the French and Dutch people rejecting the proposed EU constitution in 2005.

Again and again, we find that at the heart of the reaction against globalization is a dedication to local identities. For example, people in Europe are finding it very difficult—impossible so far—to move from "I am English" "I am French" "I am Italian" "I am German" and so on, to "I am European." What kind of a person is a European exactly? Nobody so far seems to be able to give a satisfactory answer. The European identity is in the minds of intellectuals, but not in the hearts of ordinary Europeans. There is no passion when Europeans talk about European identity; as yet, Europeans are not ready to die for the European flag and their sentiments remain fiercely tied to the local. It is still at the local level that identities are forged.

The same passionate drive that leads the Scots, the Catalanians, the Serbians, the Kurds, and countless other minority groups to strive for an authentic identity, is leading Muslim communities to rethink the kinds of people they are and what they are becoming. Like numerous other minorities, Muslim communities are questioning the impact of globalization. The sheer speed, size, and sweep of globalization forces are leading to a sense of powerlessness. It is local identities that can serve as anchors, helping to stabilize individuals and groups as the massive tides of change sweep past.

Within the increasingly global economy, people are primarily concerned with membership in relatively smaller units: nation, city, or village, rather than world, continent, or regional economic bloc. When they ask the question, what sort of person am I? They are far less likely to answer abstractly that "I am a human being" or "I am a European" or "I am African," and far more likely to respond by asserting "I am English," or "I attend mosque Y," or "My family is Z," or by identification with some other tangible group.

In some cases, identity is anchored on religious affiliation or association with a sports team, or some other entity with appeal beyond national borders, and it could be claimed that such identification is global rather than local. For example, it could be claimed that a person who identifies himself firstly as a Muslim or as a fan of Manchester United is "thinking globally"—after all, the appeal of both Islam and Manchester United is global. But this is not a valid claim, because in such cases identification is with only some people around the world—such as those who happen to agree with one's interpretation of Islam and those who support the same soccer team—to the exclusion of others. Far from being a global identity, it is a partisan affiliation with a narrow band of particular others. Manchester United fans expressed intense hatred toward an American, an "outsider," who bought a majority share in "their" English soccer club in 2005, just as Salafi Muslims cast insults (and in some cases, bullets and bombs) at Shi'a Muslims, who they see as outsiders.

The continued tendency for people to identify with local rather than global groups has a long history and may have evolutionary roots. Plato's Republic was designed to be a very small society, and modern societies that become very large tend to be organized on the basis of much smaller units, such as states (in America), provinces (in Canada and France), counties (in UK), and the like. Even in enormous urban centers such as New York City, identification takes place with neighborhoods and other smaller units within cities. In our evolutionary past, survival would have been enhanced among people who showed a preference for groups that were cohesive and smaller in size, so that group members were able to identify and cooperate with one another more effectively. The upper size limit of human hunter-gatherer groups was probably several hundred individuals, depending on the season of the year. Experiences in modern institutions, particularly schools, suggest that problems of cohesion and discipline tend to increase when the institution is several thousand rather than several hundred in size.[12]

Consequently, the push toward globalization, associated as it is with integration into larger and larger units, might make sense economically, but it runs against the human tendency to want to identify with local groups, places, and events. The transition from smaller to larger identity units took centuries to evolve in Western societies, but is being pushed through quickly in the third world, creating enormous tensions and conflicts. Moreover, the larger identity units available in third world societies, such as those based in Islam, are themselves under pressure to change to fit modern, global standards. The result at the level of individual experience is further tensions and paradoxes. It is in this larger context of global tensions and paradoxes that we must view the evolution of terrorism. In discussing this evolution, I use a staircase metaphor.

THE STAIRCASE TO TERRORISM

I begin by envisaging terrorism as the final step on a narrowing staircase. This is what I call the "staircase to terrorism." Of course, in this context we are more used to associating staircases with the tragedy of the Twin Towers. On September 11, 2001, hundreds of firefighters heroically plunged into the flaming Twin Towers of the World Trade Center in New York City to help people trapped inside. The story of how firefighters fought their way up the smoke-filled stairs to reach injured and traumatized victims is now part of American lore and legend. Three hundred and forty-three firefighters lost their lives on those stairs; the firefighters were still pounding their way up step-by-step to comfort the multitudes who cried out for help when the Towers collapsed.

During the moving ceremonies that followed the tragedy of September 11, the firefighters were justifiably showered with high tributes. In the midst of the tear-filled ceremonies, prayers, and dedications that celebrated the heroism of the firefighters, one could hear the echoes of anguished cries and voices that filled the Twin Towers' staircases. The physical effigy of the Twin Towers had collapsed to the ground, but for many people the spirit of the firefighters kept on climbing and soared beyond the highest points of this world.

Seemingly on a different planet, the suicide terrorists who piloted hijacked civilian aircrafts into the Twin Towers had reached the final steps on a very different staircase, one that remains hidden from view for most people, particularly in the West. This is the staircase to terrorism, and tragically it stands even stronger and more solid today than ever before.

The "heroic" staircase to terrorism will only be understood through empathy, perseverance, and self-control, particularly because of the explosive emotional questions still lingering. From asking: "Why do they hate us?" Americans in particular must move on to gain insights into why from the perspective of many millions of people around the world, the staircase to terrorism is associated with as much heroism, honor, and self-sacrifice as the staircase climbed by New York firefighters on September 11. Difficult and gut-wrenching as it feels, we must come to understand why so many people around the world are sympathetic toward the terrorists' point of view.

From the terrorists' point of view, the act of terrorism is at the very end, not the beginning, of the story of terrorism. To begin at the beginning from the terrorists' point of view is to tell the story of how the adult terrorist began life as you and I started life, like any other child, playing and learning to adapt to a changing world. There is nothing in the biological makeup of the person to cause him or her to become a terrorist. We must look to the environment to explain terrorism, and we must ask questions about the environment of societies that nurture terrorism.

What is it about an environment that can teach a child to eventually look at the world from the terrorists' point of view? This is a vast mystery to most people, because the terrorists' point of view condones threatening, injuring, and even killing civilians, bystanders, and people who are just peacefully going about their ordinary daily lives. These civilians are not a threat to the terrorist—they are not armed, or even engaged in political activity. Why should the terrorist see them as an enemy and see it justified to terrorize, injure, or kill them? These questions demand answers.

The answer that I provide has to do with the psychological core of a human being: *identity*, our conception of the sort of person we are and how we are valued. Identity is based on cognition, but perhaps even more importantly it is based on emotions, such as shame and anger. Emotions are integral to our identities: we do not see ourselves and the groups we belong to objectively; rather, we tend to have biased perceptions and emotions about ourselves and the groups we belong to.

The staircase to terrorism involves transformations in identity, as a person moves from floor to floor. By the time a person has moved from the ground floor to the top of the building, he or she has changed identity in ways that are deep enough to allow for the destruction of the self and others.

CHAPTER 3

The Staircase to Terrorism

WHY DID THE UNITED STATES SUPPORT OSAMA BIN LADEN?

It was 1982 and I was in Baluchestan, in a region where the national borders of Iran, Afghanistan, and Pakistan drift into one another, sometimes completely disappearing in sandstorms and the perpetual movements of tribal people, drug smugglers, and the seemingly neverending flow of refugees. The Soviet invasion of Afghanistan in 1979 had created an enormous humanitarian crisis, with millions of refugees pouring across the borders from Afghanistan in the north into Iran, and Pakistan in the south, away from the control of the Soviet military. I was participating in a World Food Programme (WFP) project to help feed and supply displaced Afghanis now huddled together in the exploding refugee camps.

Ostensibly the enormous numbers of Afghani refugees were being helped by national and international agencies for purely humanitarian reasons, but the larger, unwritten goal bankrolled by the West and a number of oil-rich Islamic states was the fight against communism. Russia's historic ambition to reach the waters of the Persian Gulf seemed even more of a threat to both Western powers and local Islamic regimes, now that Moscow was controlled by communist ideologues. So the Afghani refugees were fed, armed, trained, and sent back up north to fight and to eventually drive the Soviets out of Afghanistan (the strength of the Islamic resistance and insurgency in the face of the Soviet military was an early warning and indicator of the continued resistance U.S. forces would later face in Iraq and Afghanistan).

The region had already experienced historic changes during the 1970s, and there was anxious expectation of more dizzying political, economic, and social changes to come. The 1978–1979 revolution in Iran had ousted the pro-American dictator, the last Shah, brought a fundamentalist Islamic government into power in Iran, and thousands of Islamic fundamentalists from different countries in the region had mobilized and banded in this area to help fight the Soviet "infidels" in Afghanistan. I had no idea at the time that Osama bin Laden and some of his chief aides, including Ayman al-Zawahiri who was to play a leading role in the anti-American insurgency in post-Saddam Iraq, were among the Islamic army in Afghanistan, but I was well aware that Saudi money and fighters were pouring into the area.

The talk among many Western diplomats was that the only way to defeat the communists was to feed the fires of fundamentalist Islam. A few wise heads wondered what all this would lead to in the future, but the urgent problem at hand, the communist threat, drowned out these faint questioning voices. On the streets the air was filled with cries of "Allah Akbar" (God is Great) and the United States in particular was eager to help Osama bin Laden and other Islamic fundamentalists rush up north to fight the Soviets.

The Enemy of My Enemy

The most striking feature of the situation in Afghanistan in the 1980s was not that American, Saudi, and other Arab, and even Iranian support was combining to help Islamic fundamentalists defeat communist forces. After all, the very broad coalition to fight communism could be explained through the ancient slogan "the enemy of my enemy is my ally"—Iran, America, and the Arab States were far from being the best of friends, but all shared an enemy in the Soviet Union. Much more striking was another trend highlighted by events in Afghanistan: the world was truly becoming a global village—no group or nation could act as an island in the new global village. Even events in the most "distant" lands such as Afghanistan had to be given serious attention by the rest of the world.

But, unfortunately, the U.S. government neglected this important lesson of globalization. After the Mujahedeen drove Soviet forces out of Afghanistan in 1989, the United States stopped paying attention to the enormous numbers of Islamic fundamentalists it had directly nurtured in the region. One outcome was the coming to power of the fanatical Taliban regime in Afghanistan, which provided a haven for Al Qaeda and a platform to perpetrate the tragedy of September 11. Another outcome was the strengthening of fundamentalism in Pakistan, and the growth of training grounds to prepare "Islamic freedom fighters" (the

Indian government would call them "terrorists") to fight against communism and secularism (and also for the independence of Kashmir from India).

The same religious zeal stoked up in Pakistan to fight communists has been used to fight wars against neighboring India. Pakistan gained independence from India on the basis of an "Islamic identity," and the crisis of identity experienced by Muslims globally has had a profound impact on Pakistani society. The growth of Islamic terrorism in Kashmir is one manifestation of this. On the one hand there is the growth of a secular, professional, educated, and relatively liberal middle-class in Pakistan. This class tends toward democracy and away from orthodox Islam. On the other hand, there is a backlash against secularism by fundamentalists determined to return to "pure," "unadulterated" Islam, as it was assumed to have been practiced by the founders 1,400 years ago.

Was the U.S. support for Islamic fundamentalists in the Near and Middle East during the late 1960s and 1970s justified? On the one hand it was justified, because Islamic movements grew to form a "green belt" on the southern borders of the Soviet Union, preventing the spread of communism in countries such as Afghanistan, Iran, and Pakistan. In part because of Islamic resistance, the Soviets never achieved their historic goal of reaching the waters of the Persian Gulf and the Arabian Sea. The war in Afghanistan proved to be a lethal drain on Soviet resources, just as the war against Muslim Chechnia continues to drain Russian resources in the third millennium. I have heard some American analysts argue that despite September 11 and all that has happened, U.S. support for Islamic fundamentalism and even Osama bin Laden was justified because it helped to destroy the Soviet empire. According to this thinking, the United States should now increase its support for Islamic fundamentalist and "breakaway" movements in Western China, as a way of weakening the grip of the Chinese communist authorities.

Some would go further and argue that an external threat is needed to help mobilize the American population and keep it focused on the superpower role of the country. These people would agree with Sigmund Freud, who proposed that you can bind individuals together in love, as long as there are some left over to hate as outsiders. Islamic fundamentalism has taken the place of the Soviets in playing the role of "the outsiders to hate." Of course, China is rising fast and may fill this outsider role within the next few decades. According to this view, then, there must always be a hated out-group, otherwise America will become "soft," lose focus, and stop being a capitalist powerhouse. Supporters of probusiness groups and conservative causes have benefited from the external threat posed by Islamic fundamentalism, because it led to stronger support for President Bush and right-wing, "entrepreneurial" politicians generally.

A basic principle of group dynamics is that external threat leads to internal group cohesion and support for more aggressive, assertive leadership. There are numerous examples of aggressive, single-minded political leaders who come to power as a result of external threat and at times of war, but fade with the disappearance of external threat and the transition to peace. Winston Churchill, the Prime Minister of Britain during World War Two (1939–1945), is the quintessential example. Churchill was a conservative British politician who was unrivaled as a leader when his country was at war, but faded quickly during peace. The same kind of "rally behind the leader" mentality helped George W. Bush win a second term in office as President of the United States. Thus, from one perspective, U.S. support for Islamic fundamentalism not only helped defeat the Soviets, but also helped mobilize Americans behind an aggressive, probusiness leader who could ensure American global supremacy.

On the other hand, the long-term costs and consequences of U.S. support for Islamic fundamentalism is not clear yet. The United States has entered the twenty-first century engaged in an economically draining and politically divisive international fight against Islamic fundamentalism, with no clear end in sight. The presence of "victorious" U.S. troops in Iraq and Afghanistan has increased anti-American sentiment, inside and outside Islamic countries around the world. Although the outcome of these processes is not clear, one thing that is very clear is that the twenty-first century world will not allow any country to remain isolated from the international consequences of its own actions.

THE "GOOD COPY PROBLEM"

The global village is now a reality, and I could see clear signs of that emerging reality in Afghan refugee camps during the early 1980s. Transistor radios available everywhere in the camps transmitted news from multiple sources, and like everyone else in that situation I got used to listening to radio B.B.C., radio America, as well as a host of local stations. Television was less available, but even at that time I ran into people in refugee camps who asked me about the latest American soap opera shows. Young people, often the majority in the camps, were the most eager to have news about Western pop culture. Even as they cried out "Allah Akbar!" and went off to fight the infidel communists, young Afghans were also magnetized by the pull of American culture and Hollywood.

Of course, when I refer to "young people," in the context of the Near and Middle East I mean "most people," because the young are the numerical majority. Population growth in most parts of the Near and Middle East has been steaming ahead at between 3 and 4 percent per annum; keep in mind that only a growth rate of 2.1 percent is needed to maintain a population level. In practical terms, high population growth rate has meant that most Near and Middle East countries doubled their population between 1970 and 2000. This is in sharp contrast to the situation in many industrialized societies, where the native population growth rate is below 2.1 percent; Germany, Japan, and Russia are expected to shrink in population during the first half of the twenty-first century. Whereas the industrialized countries are characterized by aging and static or shrinking native populations, the countries of the Near and Middle East have to cope with exploding population levels, with at least 60 percent of the people being below twenty-one years of age. Authorities tend to focus on the material needs of this young population, but the young also have profound identity needs, and this is particularly true of the young in Islamic societies.

Islamic Youth Experience an Identity Crisis

My experiences among Afghan refugees underscored a profound reality I had already confronted during my time in revolutionary Iran and in some other Islamic regions, as well as among Muslim communities in Western Europe and North America: the young in Islamic communities have been experiencing a deep identity crisis. This crisis has three essential features.

First, the crisis is taking place in the midst of dramatic political, economic, and cultural changes. The young in Islamic societies find themselves caught in a whirlwind of multilevel changes, so powerful and widespread that they throw individuals around like helpless straw in a tornado. Revolutions, war, mass migration of populations, vast economic and social transformations—these form the backdrop to the identity crisis of the young in the Islamic world.

Second, Muslim youth gripped by this crisis are eagerly searching for signposts to guide them toward a better tomorrow. The young always look to the future, and to ideals and models that can feed their dreams of a better tomorrow. Where are such ideals and models to come from in the Islamic world? Unfortunately the two models that are most readily available, put forward by Western culture and by Islamic fundamentalists, are both highly unsuitable.

Third, increasing Americanization and the importation of Western ideals to the Islamic world has led many youth in Islamic societies to be attracted to Western ideals of woman and man, only to experience the "good copy problem" as a result. This problem is subtle and complex, and is at the heart of the identity crisis of Muslim youth.

The "good copy problem" has its roots in the ideal of woman and man propagated by Hollywood and the Western media. Through an overwhelming flow of films, music, magazines, radio and television shows, and countless other sources, Hollywood ideals have been established on a worldwide scale.

Of course, the "good copy problem" is not only impacting Islamic societies, but is clearly visible in all non-Western societies, even industrial giants like Japan and superpowers of the future like China. One of the most obvious signs of this is the pervasiveness of advertising for plastic surgery in both Japan and China. The target of this advertising is invariably Japanese and Chinese women, and the message of the advertising is very direct and clear: you need to model yourself after the ideal Western woman. Toward this goal, plastic surgery procedures of increasingly drastic nature have become usual. The less drastic procedures include surgery to change the shape of the eye, to become more round, and to sculpture facial bones and particularly the jaw, to become less angular and more Western looking. The more drastic procedures include adding several inches to the length of legs, through tortuous surgery and treatment that sometimes takes months and even years—all this to become a "good copy" of an idealized Western model.

If the pressure on Japanese and Chinese people is so great to copy the Western model, the pressure felt by people in Islamic societies is even greater because militarily and economically, as well as in terms of leadership, Islamic societies are far weaker.

The message from the Westernized Islamic elites is clear: the best that youth from Islamic societies can achieve is to become a "good copy" of Western ideals; they can never be as good or better than the original Western models. This has created a void, an opportunity for alternative ideals to make an impact. The Westernized elites of the Islamic world have been unable to fill this void, because they have themselves been engrossed in the quest to become "good copies" of Western models of the ideal woman and man. These Westernized elites are not seen as authentic or credible. Surprising as it may seem, so far the most viable candidates for filling this void in the lives of youth in Islamic societies have been Islamic fundamentalists.

THE APPEAL OF ISLAMIC FUNDAMENTALISM IN THE WIDER WORLD

To understand the wider appeal of Islamic fundamentalists in modern Muslim societies, we have to step back and review two apparently contradictory trends around the globe.

On the one hand the global village is becoming a reality and the world is becoming a much smaller place. Improved transportation and communications systems, enormous migrations involving hundreds of millions of immigrants and refugees moving across national and even continental boundaries, modern media, and electronic communications—these have contributed to the global village becoming a reality.

On the other hand, we witness the birth or reappearance of hundreds of separatist movements, people trying to break away from the larger group to create their own, smaller unit. There are clear signs of this separatist trend in both the industrialized and the developing societies, from the establishment of a Scottish Parliament by Scottish nationalists to the Free Aceh Movement, sometimes referred to as the Aceh Sumatra National Liberation Front (ASNLF), in Indonesia, from the Basques separatists in Spain to Kurdish separatists in Turkey, Iran, and Iraq, from Quebec nationalists wanting to break away from English Canada to Sikh separatists in India—in every part of the globe we find movements involving people attempting to reorganize their lives as part of smaller units.

Separatist movements appear to be swimming against the strong economic current of globalization. For example, at the same time that Welsh nationalists are striving to revive the Welsh language and rekindle feelings of Welsh nationalism, Wales is becoming more integrated into an expanding European Union that has all but officially recognized English as the common language of Europe. At the same time that Quebec separatists are fighting to gain independence from English Canada, the Canadian economy and culture is being integrated into a larger American economy and culture, in part through the NAFTA (North American Free Trade Agreement). Similarly, the struggle of Sikh separatists in India, Tamil Separatists in Sri Lanka, Aceh separatists in Indonesia, and hundreds of other similar "independence" movements seems to be going against the strong tide of global economic and cultural integration. The world seems to be shrinking and the signals are too striking to ignore.

Managers of international organizations can now move to different company affiliates in Hong Kong, Beijing, Los Angeles, London, Delhi, Istanbul, and numerous other major urban centers around the world without experiencing serious changes in their lifestyles. The same type of houses, schools, cars, television shows, music, books, food, and countless goods and services will be available in all of these locations. Morever, they will work in the same international business language, English. For the first time in human history, two world powers, Great Britain followed by the United States, have used and propagated the same language.

The Death of Local Languages

The rapid death of minority languages and the increasing worldwide dominance of a few languages is another clear indication of globalization trends.[13] The number of living languages has decreased by over a half since the time Columbus arrived in the New World, from around

15,000 to around 6,000 today. By the end of the twenty-first century, most of the 6,000 living languages will have disappeared. Languages are being lost at a rate of at least two or three a month. Hundreds of languages only have one or a few speakers left alive, while about 96 percent of the world's languages are spoken by about 4 percent of the world's population. At the other extreme, about 2.5 billion people speak the four most "popular" languages: Mandarin Chinese (1 billion speakers), English (600 million speakers), Hindustani (500 million speakers), and Spanish (400 million speakers). In academic, political, and business spheres, English is now the global language.

Although in most domains globalization does not just mean Americanization, in education globalization does mean Americanization. Higher education around the globe has been invaded not only by the English language, but also by Americanization generally. Educational institutions in most countries are changing to adapt to the American model, and this is happening even in Europe where universities have a far longer tradition than in the United States. An example is the Americanization of the universities in the United Kingdom where I studied. Each time I return to the United Kingdom, I notice the universities have taken on more American characteristics. For example, the kinds of national ranking systems of institutions and departments, and grant seeking activities, which were frowned upon in the United Kingdom as "American commercialism," are now followed religiously by British academics.

The Americanization of higher education around the world is even more clearly apparent in the material actually taught in classes. The American textbook industry sets the pace for the rest of the world, and many countries use American texts (mostly translated to the local language) in their university classes. Of course, students in such classes tend to follow American trends in the clothing they wear, the music they listen to, the films they watch, and the books they read. Students are also highly motivated to learn English, because progress in school depends a great deal on their English proficiency, rather than proficiency in local languages.

Several personal experiences have highlighted for me the ironies and paradoxes of the Americanization of higher education around the world. During my work in Iranian universities after the 1978–1979 revolution, I developed a proposal for a basic psychology text in Farsi that would introduce students to alternatives to mainstream Western (American dominated) psychology. Unfortunately, I failed to win support for this proposal from the authorities. It seems my proposal was not politically correct in the context of Islamic Iran. Time passed, and in order to be able to remain active in research and to publish I moved to the West, working first at McGill University in Canada and then at Georgetown University in Washington, D.C. When I visited Iran fifteen years later,

I was curious to see what "revolutionary" texts were being used in the main universities. To my surprise, I discovered that the books being used were (and continue to be!) either direct translations of American texts, or books that are very closely modeled on American texts.

What Sort of Person Am I? The Importance of Authenticity

"What sort of person am I?" This is the most important question humans ask. The answer individuals give to this question shapes everything they think and do. The ability to answer the question "What sort of person am I" in a satisfactory way is essential to healthy adult functioning. We need to think carefully about what "satisfactory" means in this context.

In the West, researchers have emphasized the need for a positive and distinct identity. "Positive" means that people should evaluate me favorably, they should see me in a good light (recall the discussion on Social Identity Theory in Chapter 2). "Distinct" refers to the idea that I should be seen as being in some important way different from others. These are important criteria, and they make a lot of sense in the Western context. In a global context and particularly in the context of Islamic societies, however, another criterion has even broader relevance for evaluating identity: authenticity.

In Western societies, the criterion of authenticity has not become prominent in assessing identity, in large part because Western societies are in the lead and set the pace for non-Westerners; Westerners are the ones being copied rather than the ones copying others. Questions about authenticity are more likely to arise for groups, such as Islamic societies, which are "forced" by various factors to model their own identity after that of other groups.

Islamic societies are experiencing a vast cultural invasion, particularly from the West, in the shape of cultural elements, including films, music, clothing, architecture, technology, and also educational systems, values, beliefs, morals, and gender roles. More and more cultural elements are being imported to Islamic societies, mostly from the West, and this trend seems to be getting stronger. When individuals in Islamic societies ask the crucial question "What sort of person am I?" their main challenge is to find some kind of authentic identity, one that has not been imported and shaped for them by the West, India, China, and the rest of the world.

Unfortunately the leadership of Islamic societies has not been successful in providing constructive models for their populations to follow. There has not been a Mahatma Gandhi or a Nelson Mandela in the Islamic world. The nationalist leaders, the most effective probably being Nasser in Egypt, made little headway in establishing either authentic identities or democratic societies. The nationalist leaders who showed more promise and had stronger democratic tendencies, such as Mossadeq in Iran, were quickly removed from the scene by the intervention of Western powers. The failure of nationalist leaders to help provide authentic identities in Islamic societies left a vacuum, into which have stepped Islamic fundamentalists.

Authentic Identity in Islamic Societies

The most important reason why Khomeini and other Islamic fundamentalists have been able to mobilize Islamic societies in a way that nationalists could not, is the authentic identity fundamentalists offer Islamic people. This authentic identity is presented as being untainted by Western biases. The "back to our true roots" message of fundamentalists is highly effective not only in mobilizing support, but also damning the two groups that could rival fundamentalists for leadership: first, the nationalists and second, leaders such as the Saudis who can be attacked as "Western puppets" despite their "Islamic front."

One reason why Western analysts have neglected the importance of authentic identity in Islamic societies is that they have worked on the assumption that Islamic people would be happy to strive to become "good copies" of the West. It should have occurred to analysts that striving to become a "good copy" would result in inadequate self-esteem. It is rather odd that in Western contexts so much importance has been given to self-esteem, but in evaluating the situation in Islamic societies Westerners have neglected self-esteem.

I do not mean by this that people should be encouraged to develop an inflated view of themselves.[14] Unfortunately the "self-esteem movement" has created more problems than it has solved, particularly in schools, by encouraging the development of children with inflated self-esteem. Slogans such as "everyone is a star," now plastered on the walls of schools, can lead to serious problems, particularly for underachieving children. Individuals who can barely read and write, or solve the most basic math problems, are growing up in schools that encourage them to think they are stars. This is hardly a good strategy to encourage children to try harder. In asking, "What sort of person am I?" the underachieving child arrives at a very unsatisfactory answer: "I'm a star, but I don't do well in tests, I'm looked down on, and I can't get a decent job in the larger world." Associated with these feelings of inadequacy is the rage and violence that characterizes life in many inner cities in America.

True, economic and cultural enclaves and neighborhoods can serve to buffer individuals against the harsher realities of the world. Underachieving individuals living in poor neighborhoods can compare themselves mostly or only with others around them, and maintain a positive self-esteem that way. However, the larger world will insist on inserting itself into the lives of even the most insular enclaves, not only through the media but particularly through the job market and economic realities. If I am unskilled, almost illiterate, and poor, I may compare myself to others who are equally badly off or even worse off in order to make myself feel better, but as soon as I step outside my enclave and try to improve my situation, the harsh realities of the wider world will come crashing down on me.

But at least the poor, the unskilled, the less powerful in America can revert to national pride when they answer the question "What sort of person am I?" The slogan "America is number one!" is proclaimed by economically poor and poorly educated Whites, African Americans, and Hispanic army recruits as they march away to defend "American interests" around the globe. Indeed, working-class and middle-class America is prone to be far more patriotic, and to rely on national pride as a source of their identities, far more than the American rich, who invest their money in China and other places where there is greatest profits, rather than investing in America out of patriotic fervor. Irrespective of personal status, the American population has "America," the "land of opportunity," to be proud of.

The American genius is that for so long, the few have persuaded the many that America really is an ideal worth sacrificing for, even though the benefits of American success disproportionally benefit the few.

The success of America is clearly through co-opting the many to work for national goals; a lesson not yet learned by the leadership in Islamic countries, among other places. By "co-opting" I do not mean something sinister; rather, I mean training people to believe that, first, they have a say in how decisions are made and, second, that there is turn-taking in sharing power. Regular elections and term limits in holding certain positions (e.g., the U.S. President can be in power for a maximum of eight years) effectively serve to co-opt the population in America.

It is the cultural context of the United States, particularly the pervasive ideology of the American Dream, that enables the American elite, the "haves," to co-opt the nonelite, the "have nots," to feel pride in America. Context is also of paramount importance in shaping the beliefs of individuals in Islamic societies. The staircase metaphor is designed to keep our focus on the context in which terrorism takes place.

THE STAIRCASE TO TERRORISM AND CULTURE

Envisage a narrowing staircase leading to the terrorist act at the top of a multistory building.[15] We all begin life on the ground floor of the building. At this stage, the future terrorist is no different from you or I. The staircase leads to higher and higher floors, and whether a person remains on a particular floor depends on the doors and spaces that she or he imagines will open to her or him on that floor. The fundamentally important feature of the situation is not only the actual number of floors, stairs, rooms, and so on, but how people perceive the building and the doors they think are open to them. As individuals climb the winding and darkening staircase, they see fewer and fewer choices, until the only possible outcome is the destruction of others, or oneself, or both.

Is the staircase to terrorism the same for all cultures? Yes, the staircase is the same in terms of the source of terrorism being the conditions on the ground floor and other lower floors. This is its most important universal feature, and it has vital implications for combating terrorism in the long term. In all cultures, terrorism can only be defeated in the long term if conditions on the ground floor are reformed.

A second consistency across cultures is that when a terrorist reaches the fourth or higher floors, there is little possibility of his or her climbing back down the staircase. This is because on the highest floors the influence of context is so strong and the push toward the top of the staircase so powerful that only rarely can an individual move back down.

But the staircase to terrorism is also in some key respects different across cultures. One such difference is in terms of the distance between the floors on the staircase, indicating the amount of time it will take for people to move from one floor to another. The distance between floors could change over time within a particular society. For example, after the invasion of Iraq by U.S.-led forces in 2003, cultural conditions in Iraq were such that movement from the ground floor to the first, second, third, fourth, and fifth floors was rapid. Within a year, thousands of people had moved from the ground level all the way up to the top of the staircase to terrorism. The presence of non-Muslim "invaders" in Iraq was one factor that led to the shrinking of the distance between floors.

Another cross-cultural difference is in terms of the importance of each floor and the salience of psychological processes characteristic of each floor. For example, in postwar Iraq, the second floor is of the highest importance, because it is characterized by the psychological process of displaced aggression. Terrorists in postwar Iraq derive a lot of their inspiration from displacement of aggression onto U.S. military forces. In the context of Saudi Arabia, disengagement from the morality of mainstream society and engagement in a morality supporting terrorism against the Saudi regime is relatively more important than displacement of aggression.

To understand those who climb to the terrifying top of the staircase and come to see the world from the terrorists' point of view, we must first comprehend the enormous and increasing level of frustration and dissatisfaction among the hundreds of millions of people down at the ground level.

CHAPTER 4

Ground Floor: Growing Dissatisfaction among the Multitudes

Terrorists are made, they are not born. Terrorism arises from societal conditions, not individual characteristics.

But it would be far too simplistic to interpret "societal conditions" in a purely materialistic manner. The most important aspect of societal conditions is how people answer basic questions about their identities, both personal and collective. Questions about personal identity ("What sort of person am I? Am I valued? Am I listened to? Do I matter?") are answered through the filter of questions about collective identity ("What sort of group do I belong to ? Is my group valued? Is my group listened to? Does my group matter?").

Our exploration of the roots of terrorism begins with the characteristics of collective life. To understand why some individuals climb all the way up the staircase to terrorism and eventually commit terrifying acts that destroy both themselves and others, we must start by carefully looking at the conditions for collective life on the ground floor. It is on the ground floor that everyone begins, and it is on the ground floor that the vast majority of people remain, even when they feel the sharp pain of injustice and intolerance.

The ground floor of the staircase to terrorism is occupied by hundreds of millions of people. Like you and I, these people eat, drink, sleep, enjoy family life, make and break friendships, fall in love, have children, celebrate marriages, make plans, strive to improve their living conditions, try to control events in their lives, and experience feelings of justice and injustice. Most importantly, like you and I, these people are profoundly concerned about their identities and values ascribed to their identities. It is on the ground floor that millions of people arrive at understandings of themselves and their groups, and form identities, both personal and collective.

The most important feature of the ground floor is how people feel about, and how they subjectively interpret, their personal and collective identities and situations. It is the perceived rather than the actual that is most important.

THE PRIMACY OF THE PSYCHOLOGICAL

Osama bin Laden was a millionaire when he masterminded the tragedy of September 11.[16] Those who actually carried out the attacks of September 11 were from relatively affluent backgrounds, and also well educated relative to the rest of the population of their home societies. In the West Bank and Gaza, Palestinians with more years of education tend to show greater support for armed attacks against Israeli targets. In Northern Ireland, members of the Irish Republican Army have tended to be "intelligent and astute," rather than "mindless hooligans."[17] Captured members of Al Qaeda have tended not to be from the lowest economic and educational backgrounds. Indeed, Al Qaeda sympathizers and activists are often from "surprisingly" high economic and educational backgrounds. These facts highlight an important point: terrorism is explained by *perceptions* of deprivation, by *feelings* of being treated unfairly, by a *subjective* sense of injustice, rather than by objective conditions, including poverty and low education.

Relative Deprivation

What matters most is how individuals feel about their situation relative to particular others, how deprived they feel subjectively and in a comparative sense, rather than how they are doing according to objective criteria (recall our discussion of relative deprivation in Chapter 2). Of course, by emphasizing how people see the situation and how they feel, I do not mean to imply that actual material conditions do not matter. Rather, I am highlighting a rift that often exists between subjective experiences and objective conditions; how people experience a situation and what the situation is actually like; how people feel they are valued and their actual treatment.

Because there is often a rift between feelings of deprivation and material conditions, it is not always possible to change subjective feelings by altering material conditions. For example, if a group of people feel relatively deprived, it is not necessarily the case that such feelings of deprivation can be ended by improving material conditions. A great deal depends on who is selected as the comparison target. Consider the case of group A, who feel deprived in comparison with group B. The material conditions are improved for group A, so that they catch up or get closer to group B. However, group A might still feel very badly off, if its members can be induced to make upward comparisons of themselves to group C. To personalize this situation: I will feel less deprived if my income increases to compare well with other professors, but I will still feel deprived if my comparison group shifts from university professors to business executives. As this example illustrates, much depends on one's position *relative* to particular comparison targets.

The important role of relative deprivation was first systematically examined during the Second World War (1939–1945). Researchers were stumped by an unexpected series of findings. For example, although the rate of promotions was higher in the Air Corps than in some other military units, members of the Air Corps expressed less satisfaction. Such unexpected findings were explained through the concept of relative deprivation: the higher rate of promotion in the Air Corps raised expectations among all or most Air Corps members, and led to disappointment among those who were not promoted. In military units where promotions were less prevalent, expectations were generally lower and there was less of a tendency to feel relative deprivation when others were promoted.

Recall from our earlier discussions (Chapter 2) that feelings of relative deprivation can be *egoistical*, experienced with respect to an individual's personal situation relative to other individuals, or *fraternal*, involving feelings of deprivation associated with the situation of one's group relative to other groups. In the Islamic world, feelings of fraternal deprivation should be considered in the historical context of the Near and Middle East. Thus, the commonly heard narrative of collective deprivation needs to be considered in the context of a larger historical narrative.

Historical Context

The twentieth century was one long disappointment for Muslims in the Near and Middle East. Again and again, foreign powers put into place and manipulated despotic rulers in order to extend their own influence in the region. Again and again, "educated" elites perpetuated inequalities and failed to provide leadership toward more open, democratically inclined, social systems. Again and again, the hopes of the multitudes on the ground floor were dashed, even though the discovery of oil brought the promise of a significantly improved quality of life for the masses. But it was not to be. When the twentieth century came to a close, even the more "progressive" Islamic countries of the region such as Egypt, Iran, and Pakistan, which had earlier shown signs of moving toward democracy, were now firmly back in the grip of dictatorship: Mobarak in Egypt, the mullahs in Iran, and Mosharaf in Pakistan ruled with an iron fist and gave local populations no voice in decision making. Unfortunately foreign powers routinely intervened directly or indirectly to strengthen the position of dictators, rather than to encourage democracy.

At the start of the twentieth century, the decline of the Ottoman Empire and the First World War (1914–1918) created further opportunities for Britain, France, and Russia to try to extend their influence in the Near and Middle-East region. The British supported Arab rebellions, adventurously led by Lawrence of Arabia, against the declining Ottoman Empire. But rather than result in true independence for Arabs, Ottoman control was quickly replaced by British control in an area that is modern Iraq, Egypt, and Palestine, and French control in Lebanon and Syria. In a set of British and French directed maneuvers that involved a series of Arab and Persian leaders being guided through musical chairs of thrones in the region, the Saudi family gained control of Islam's holiest city, Mecca, and proclaimed the Kingdom of Saudi Arabia (1932), Faisal became King of Iraq (a country he had not even visited before!), Abdullah became King of Jordan (1923), and Reza Khan became the Shah of Iran (1926).

Whereas in the late nineteenth century Western powers had been interested in the Near and Middle East mainly for strategic reasons, particularly because of the Suez Canal (1869) and the route to India, rather than because of the presence of natural resources, by the 1930s the main focus of interest was the abundant petroleum (and later gas) reserves in the region. The first discoveries, in Masjed-Souleiman (Iran) in 1908, were soon followed by oil reserves of fantastic magnitudes, which brought a local elite riches far beyond of that imagined even in the fabled Arabian Nights.

By the end of the Second World War (1945), British and French forces were exhausted and their influence was replaced by American interests. American oil companies had been winning concessions in the Middle East well before the Second World War, but gradually they became the main players, particularly after the 1945 meeting of President Franklin Roosevelt and Abdul Aziz, the Saudi King. America also became the first country to recognize, and the most important backer of, the new state of Israel formed in 1948, although the idea of a homeland for Jews had first been given impetus by the British government's Balfour Declaration of 1917.

The Diabolical Triangle

The unique cultural and historical characteristics of the Near and Middle East region has led to the evolution of a *diabolical triangle*, involving: the Islamic masses, Israel, and local dictators. This diabolical triangle has prevented progress for the masses in Islamic countries in the region, because the attention and energy of the masses has been misdirected.

Israel remains the only democratic country in the Near and Middle East region. Israeli society allows for open elections, free press, an independent judiciary, and a thriving academic community engaged in world-class scholarship. Israeli society should be a natural ally for democracy in the rest of the region. However, rather than look to Israel as a source of inspiration for their own democratic aspirations, the Islamic masses look on Israel as an evil enemy. Why is this? The answer to this question lies in the role of local dictators, supported by the United States and other Western powers.

Various dictators in the Islamic societies of the Near and Middle East have used Israel as a convenient scapegoat, an evil enemy that is advertised as the source of all the ills of the region. In the name of fighting Israel, local dictators have crushed internal opposition to their corrupt regimes. Again and again, democratic tendencies have been destroyed on the flimsy excuse that the prodemocracy "rebels" are weakening the anti-Israeli front in the Islamic world.

Of course, part of the problem is that throughout its short history as a state, Israel has implemented a "land grab" policy and violated the rights of millions of Arabs. Israeli policy has made it easier for local Islamic dictators to convince the Muslim masses that they should focus their energies on the so-called "real enemy" threatening them from the outside. Throughout the twentieth century the United States and other Western powers have supported both Israel, a democracy, and local Islamic dictators—a paradoxical policy that has fanned the flames of war.

In this way, a diabolical triangle has been formed in the Near and Middle East region, each side of the triangle reinforcing and completing the other two sides. Local dictators continue to crush democratic movements on the excuse that all energy must be focused on destroying the enemy at the gates, the Israelis. The Islamic masses aspire to freedom and progress, but have come to see Israel, a democracy, as their enemy. Israel has used the prevailing turmoil to occupy more Arab land, making it easier for local dictators to vilify the Jewish state.

CONDITIONS ON THE GROUND FLOOR

Visitors to the Near and Middle East are often struck by the conspiratorial thinking style of the local people. Every event, particularly ones with negative outcomes, is scrutinized with the assumption that a foreign power, usually England or America, is manipulating and corrupting individuals and institutions from behind the scenes. Even events such as natural disasters, an earthquake for example, are routinely interpreted as reflecting the influence of Western powers. During the lead up to the revolution in Iran in 1978 and the downfall of the last Shah, a major earthquake hit Iran, causing many deaths and injuries. The word on the street in Tehran was that the Americans had caused the earthquake by exploding bombs deep underground, in a desperate attempt to divert the revolution and orchestrate the return of a pro-American dictator. A conspiratorial outlook is a central feature of conditions on the ground floor in Islamic societies of the Near and Middle East—justifiably so, locals would say, given the recent history of actions taken in the region by Western powers.

Historically, Western powers, most recently the United States, have intervened again and again to strengthen the more antidemocratic local movements and leaders in the Near and Middle East. The start of this was the C.I.A.-engineered coup in Iran that ousted the democratically elected Prime Minister Mohammed Mossadegh and brought back the Shah in 1953. Mossadegh was a forward thinking, educated, secular, nationalist. In the eyes of Western powers, his crime was that he wanted to nationalize Iranian oil. The ousting of Mossadegh did gain the United States some immediate benefits.

The C.I.A.-engineered coup against democracy in Iran assured the United States a quarter of a century (1953–1978) of rule by a pro-American Shah, but it also led to an end to direct American influence in Iran after 1979, as well as growing anti-American fundamentalism throughout the Near and Middle East. Is a larger lesson to be learned? There is, I believe, and to recognize it, we need to look more closely at conditions on the ground floor in Islamic societies.

Two factors should receive particular attention. First, in most Islamic societies all political opposition has routinely been eliminated and the only avenue for dissent is the mosque. Second, Islamic societies are what I term "living history" societies, in that they tend to look to narratives about the past rather than the future for inspiration and guidance.

The Mosque as the Only Avenue for Dissent and for Shaping Identity

In most Islamic societies, with the exception of religious activities and organizations, all avenues that have a bearing on social and political life are either completely closed or tightly controlled by governments. In the vast majority of cases, opposition political parties are illegal, and political leaders who might lead opposition groups are either in jail, or killed or, if they are very fortunate, they live in exile abroad. Television, radio, newspapers, and all other media outlets are also tightly controlled by government agencies, and any independent ones are immediately shut down if they dare to criticize the government or push for real reform.

Computer technology offers some new possibilities for opposition voices to be heard. Through electronic communications, opposition groups have more potential to organize, to communicate with each other, and to have fruitful contacts with democratic voices abroad. However, the number of people who enjoy access to advanced computer technology is still relatively small, most of these people are part of the elite establishment, and those dissidents who do have access find that government agents continually attempt to monitor and restrict their communications. In Islamic societies, as well as in China and some other politically closed systems, there is a continuing tug-of-war between government authorities trying to restrict the freedoms available through computer technology, and the freedom seekers attempting to evade government restrictions. Some governments have developed programs to try to ensure that computers do not unshackle the chains keeping their citizens tied down.

The one avenue for expression, and for identity formation, that governments in Islamic societies are unable to close down is the mosque. This was even true in Iran prior to the 1978–79 revolution, where the Shah was willing to assassinate secular opposition leaders and ban their organizations, but he did not assassinate Khomeini and he could not close down mosques in which preachers were stirring people up against his regime.

Of course, governments do attempt to control who preaches in mosques and that "agitators" are kept out. But given the lack of alternative avenues, the mosque inevitably becomes the gathering place for all kinds of disaffected individuals, particularly the young who seek to construct an appropriate identity for themselves. The tools available for identity construction in Islamic societies are of two basic types: the first are Western and lack authenticity; the second are fundamentalist interpretations of Islam and look back to the past for inspiration. A third, modern, more secular set of tools would develop and become available, but only if governments allowed for different, alternative voices to be heard.

Ensuring the Growth of Fundamentalist Islam

Question: What do you get when you eliminate the secular opposition in an Islamic society?
Answer: The coming to power of Islamic fundamentalists.

As I write these words, the classic scenario of the rise of Islamic fundamentalism is being played out in Egypt. The government of "lifetime"
President Mubarak has effectively eliminated all secular opposition, leaving only Islamic fundamentalists some freedom to compete in the political arena. The major Islamic party in Egypt, the Muslim Brotherhood, is
prohibited from competing in elections as a party. However, individuals
who obviously represent the Muslim Brotherhood have been allowed to
compete in the parliamentary elections of November–December 2005,
without declaring their party affiliations.

Because the Muslim Brotherhood represents the only means by which
Egyptian voters can cast an "opposition vote" against the government
in 2005, the Brotherhood increased its representation in the Egyptian
Parliament from fifteen to eighty-eight members. Although the pro-
Mubarak National Democratic Party has the vast majority of seats (454)
in the Egyptian Parliament, the signs are on the wall: there is a very high
possibility that the tide of Islamic fundamentalism will sweep across
Egypt. The only way to prevent this is to allow secular parties to compete and to gain political power.

Thus, given the repression of secular opposition movements in Islamic
societies, the only available tool for identity construction using indigenous resources is the mosque. Fundamentalist interpretations of Islam
have prevailed, in part because of certain historical tendencies in Islamic
societies, which (together with Israel, Japan, and some other societies)
tend to be what I call "living history" cultures.

DEAD-HISTORY CULTURES AND
LIVING-HISTORY CULTURES

In some cultures history is not "living" in the everyday lives of people:
they are "dead-history cultures." I do not mean this in the simplistic sense
of a culture not having a long or an illustrious history. Certainly, the
United States, Australia, and Canada are examples of countries that are
"new," in the sense that their recorded histories begin with the expansion
of Western colonial powers after the fifteenth century. They can't boast
of five thousand years of recorded, civilized life as one fairly recognizable,
continuous, cultural group, as can the Chinese, for example. Length of
recorded past is important, but by "dead history cultures" I am referring
to something more profound, a tendency for the past not to be important
for the present, for present and future plans to be independent from the
past, for people to see it as normal for their collective memories of history
not to influence present thoughts and actions.

Dead-history cultures socialize people to ignore the past, and sometimes even to disavow and disown the past. Immigrants to the United
States are encouraged to put aside their ethnic differences, to "melt" into

the mainstream and become part of the future-oriented society, the land of the "American Dream," which is always about what could be and what one could become, and not about what one has been.

Humongous disruptions and tragedies in American society, such as slavery and the Civil War, are treated as "dead history." The historical past is something to be celebrated in America, but kept in museums, restricted to parades, fenced off for special holiday festivals. The cultural message seems to be, "don't show me what happened yesterday, show me what is happening today," and at the individual level, the message is just as clear, "Don't show me what you did yesterday, show me what you can do now and tomorrow."

True, the United States Constitution stretches out like a dead hand from the past, attempting to maintain certain continuities in behavior. But the technological, economic, political, and cultural forces that dominate American culture are all forward looking. The entire collective gaze of American society is fixed on tomorrow.

At the level of the individual, also, the United States and other dead-history societies lead people to look forward, without linking what is happening with what has happened. The cultural message to individuals is, "what have you done lately?" implying that what you did "historically" or "yesterday" is not of importance. Dead-history societies are fast moving and have no time for individuals who want to sit on their laurels.

In contrast, "living-history cultures" live and breath the past, at both the individual and the collective levels; they keep history active in individual lives and in lived cultures, not museum cultures. The long, long past is often even more alive than the present. This is not in an abstract sense of the past being remembered by them, but in the practical sense of the long, long past being integral to their everyday thinking, activities, and living identity (as opposed to their "museum identity").

Another subtle but important point is that in living-history cultures, people are conscious of the hand of the past, and they explicitly and routinely invoke the past, such as particular historical traditions and events, to guide the present and future (this is not the same as saying that "the past influences the present" without individuals being conscious of the process; for example, as in the claim that the American experience with slavery influence twenty-first century American life without people in America realizing this influence).

If secular Western societies, and secular American society in particular, are the classic example of dead-history cultures, then Islamic societies, and particularly those of the Near-East, Middle-East, and North Africa, are clear examples of living-history cultures. In these Islamic societies, what happened 1,400 years ago is a powerful and active force in the everyday lives of individuals—sometimes even more powerful and active than what is happening today. This is not because of the formal, modern, educational system. Indeed, the formal, modern, educational system in these countries is designed to teach little history, because history is often a controversial discipline that has to be vetted or avoided so as not to offend the sensibilities of the contemporary ruling elites.

Rather than relying on formal accounts of history to transmit the past, in living-history cultures it is informal narratives, everyday stories told about the collective past, that help perpetuate and amplify the influence of history. Such narratives are part of the fabric of everyday practices. For example, in Shi'a Islam, the martyrdom of Imam Ali and the "tragedy of Karbela" is not just a tale narrated to Shi'a children so they learn how Shi'a Muslims split from the Sunni Muslims about 1,300 years ago, but it is also a story that is lived out by way of everyday practices and important ceremonies throughout the year, and also personalized in the lives of individual Shi'a Muslims. One way in which this personalization takes places is through the ceremony of *rowzeh-khani*, which serves both as a religious ceremony and a group therapy session.

The ceremony of *rowzeh-khani* is directed by a *rowzeh-khan*, a male who knows by heart a number of stories central to the history of Shi'a Islam. To succeed, the *rowzeh-khan* must have a good voice, capable of narrating and singing in emotionally moving styles. He must switch easily from being an entertainer, to being a therapist guiding a group to weep openly and to publicly express strong emotions. The success of the *rowzeh-khan* is judged in large part by how effective he is in moving the group members from one emotional state to another.

The *rowzeh-khani* is a wonderful example of a ceremony that integrates Shi'a Muslim traditions into the everyday practices of ordinary people. This ceremony usually takes place in the evening in a private home and is financed by the host, as a form of "service" that increases the piety of the host and boosts her or his chances of reaching heaven in the afterlife. Guests typically include family, friends, and neighbors, their numbers varying from half a dozen to several hundred, depending on the budget of the host. The guests sit in sex-segregated groups, usually out of sight of one another: females in one area and males in another. Food is served to guests, and throughout the meal the *rowzeh-khan* narrates tales.

The first part of the ceremony is slow moving, as guests arrive, take off their shoes as they enter the house, and take their places (usually on the floor), with the most important guests sitting at the "top" of the room, furthest away from the entrance door. The food often includes several types of rice dishes, stews with a variety of vegetables and herbs, as well as roasted chicken, and sometimes kebabs. At this stage the *rowzeh-khan* will talk in an everyday tone, not trying very hard to attract attention.

He will make a few introductory remarks about the special occasion for the *rowzeh-khani*, perhaps add a few words about the host and the people gathered, then slowly move into the narrative of a major historical tragedy (the story told is almost always a tragedy), such as the martyrdom of Imam Ali.

As the tragedy unfolds, the voice of the *rowzeh-khan* gradually becomes louder and more animated. He now demands the attention of the guests, who have come to the end of the meal and are more ready to become engaged in the narrative. The narrative is not received as a historical tale of distant events, but as a tale that is integral to the everyday lives of those present—so much so that individuals identify intensely with Imam Ali and his followers, and weep as they hear about their tragic end. The success of the *rowzeh-khan* is gauged in large part by how moved the guests are to weep.

The ceremony of *rowzeh-khani* is in some respects similar to group therapy as popularized by humanistic psychologists, particularly in the way emotions are shared and expressed. At various times during the process, the participants laugh, cry, wail, sink into the world of their own troubles, and climb out of the depths of despair, refreshed and feeling that the weights on their backs have become lighter. The climax of the ceremony is reached when the *rowzeh-khan* brings the participants to the end of the journey, the last agonies of the martyred Imam and his followers. Everyone sobs helplessly, for their own sorrows as much as for the martyrs, and the next moment the *rowzeh-khani* releases them from sadness, brings them face to face with a happy ending, with the martyrs safely placed in paradise. The participants switch in emotional experience, from deep sorrow and weeping to refreshing happiness and laughter.

The *rowzeh-khani* is one of many examples of ceremonies in Shi'a Islam, and other living-history societies, through which the historical past is integrated into the everyday present. In such societies, the past is tightly woven into personal identity through socialization processes. Rather than being a remote reference point, the past is an active signpost for present and future personal actions and values. Not surprisingly, in the search for an appropriate identity, in living-history societies the past has a strong influence on directions taken by individuals.

The reassuring aspect of the past for people in Islamic societies is that it can help them feel unique and positive about themselves. For example, the *rowzeh-khani* leaves the faithful refreshed and invigorated. They feel stronger, healthier, and better able to take up the challenges of the world. The message they receive from the past enriches them, just as leaders such as Khomeini lauded the Islamic faithful and told them that they are the best, they are spiritually superior.

This is in contrast to the message "become a good copy the West!" being received in Islamic societies from the West, and from their own Westernized elite.

EXITING THE GROUND FLOOR

From among the hundreds of millions of frustrated, dissatisfied, and ill-treated people on the ground floor in the Near and Middle East, some individuals start to climb the stairs to the first floor. These individuals are not large in number, and they are only loosely, if at all, affiliated with organized groups or movements. For the most part, these individuals are simply motivated to improve their living conditions, to find greater justice, and to achieve a more satisfactory identity for themselves. If they had been living in the West, they would have signed petitions complaining about their situation, or spoken out in local town hall meetings, or sent e-mails and letters to newspapers and to their political representatives, or taken part in a protest march. But in the countries of the Near and Middle East, such actions could land a person in jail, or worse.

Finally, before we leave the ground floor, readers might be tempted to think that the people of the Near and Middle East are unduly influenced by the imagined rather than the real state of the world, that they live too much in the psychological rather than the actual world. How else would they end up feeling that they are doing badly, when in material terms things have improved for most of them? Surely people in Saudi Arabia must see that they are far more affluent now than they have ever been, even given the very unequal distribution of oil money in the kingdom? Why are people not making judgments on the basis of actual material conditions? Why do they feel worse off, when they are better off?

In case we imagine these questions only apply to people in the Near and Middle East, we should pay attention to research in Western societies on what has been called the *Progress Paradox*, the better life gets, the worse people feel. Just because there is progress in the standard of living and health of Americans, does not mean they are feeling better off—they are feeling worse off. Research using the *Happiness Index*, reflects the same complexities between subjective feelings and actual material conditions. For example, even though the standard of living has improved in the United States over the last half century, about the same number of people feel "very happy" today as compared to the 1950s. Also, the United States routinely ranks lower than many economically poor countries on the Happiness Index. In the past, people in countries such as the Philippines and Ghana have reported higher scores on the Happiness Index than people in the United States.

So, why do people in the West not feel happier as their situation improves according to objective criteria? And why do people in the West not feel safer, as the level of actual violence declines? The most important reason is that happiness and safety are examples of experiences that depend to a large extent on subjective, psychological, interpretations. Particularly, such experiences depend a great deal on expectations. If I earn $5,000 in a year, I may feel content if I expected to earn just $4,000. However, if I earn $50,000 in a year, I may feel unhappy if I expected to earn $100,000.

Subjective assessments of our own situation are also highly influenced by the information we receive about the world, not only through our personal experiences but also through the larger society and the media in particular. For example, although the vast majority of us have not personally experienced increased violence since the tragedy of September 11, we have heard and seen endless images of violence and war through the media. Without fail every day there are headlines about people killed in fighting going on in Afghanistan, Iraq, and elsewhere. The result is that although we feel we have personally experienced little violence, we believe people in general have experienced high levels of violence.[18] The media has changed our perceptions.

The role of the international media is also of paramount importance in shaping the perceptions, expectations, and identities of people in the Near and Middle East. I do not mean in the simple sense of people actually believing what the media says, particularly in terms of news. Most people in the Near and Middle East regard the international media with great suspicion, almost with as much suspicion as they regard the highly censored media of their own countries. But outside the official news programs, the international media carries a far more subtle and powerful message: images of people living a much better life, a life we should be living; images of people enjoying fuller, more meaningful, consequential identities.

Thus, the hundreds of millions of people on the ground floor in Islamic communities are experiencing rising, unfulfilled expectations. They feel they are denied the political, economic, and social freedoms that the international media shows many other communities enjoy. The secular opposition groups in Islamic societies are severely restricted or completely banned, and the only avenue left open for any critical expression is the mosque. Consequently, religion has become the one medium through which they can attempt to mobilize and to find an authentic voice and identity.

But the world of Islam is itself in great turmoil, and there is an intense and sometimes bloody struggle to decide the way ahead according to "true" Islam. Some factions are fighting for a return to "pure" Islam, the way they believe it was practiced 1,400 years ago. Other voices are calling for an Islamic reformation, a transformation that would grant equality to women and allow Islamic societies to meet the needs of the twenty-first century. Still others are calling for Islamic societies to try to take on new identities and to become good copies of the West. In the midst of this identity crisis in the Islamic world, and the political and economic convulsions being experienced by Islamic societies, some individuals seek solutions by climbing to the next level of the staircase to terrorism. These individuals are motivated by different religious, nationalist, ethnic, and personal causes, but share a common experience: deep dissatisfaction with their identity.

CHAPTER 5

First Floor: How Do We Fight This Unfair System?

Individuals climb to the first floor and try different doors in search of solutions to what they perceive to be unjust treatment. Who are these men and women who climb up the staircase to terrorism? Are they maniacs? Troublemakers? Illiterates? The very poor? Is there something psychologically different about them? The answer is that for the most part, the individuals who climb from the ground floor to the first floor are normal people, rather like you and I. They are not particularly poor financially, or lacking education, or pathological. There is nothing that marks them as different psychologically.

Their most important characteristic is that they feel their identity is inadequate, and even what seems positive about their identity is threatened, under attack. They do not feel good about how they are seen in the larger world; they feel their voice is ignored. They are not given any significant part, even a symbolic role, in decision making, and so they climb up the staircase in search of solutions.

The solutions people seek are not just about fairness, or voice, or some abstract "rights" independent of identities. How fairly we feel we are treated, whether we are listened to, whether we see opportunities for mobility—these are all integral to our identities.

The behavior of individuals who reach the first floor is strongly influenced by how they come to answer two questions. First, are there doors that could be opened by talented persons motivated to make progress up the social hierarchy? Second, are decisions that impact on their lives made in a fair way? Do they have a voice in the decision-making process? At a deeper level, these questions come back to the issue of identity: What kind of person am I? Am I valued? What kind of group do I belong to? Is my group valued?

THE BULLETPROOF GLASS CEILING

In Western societies, women and ethnic minorities still complain about being kept down by a glass ceiling, but their situation is comfortable compared to those outside the ruling families of the Near and Middle East. The glass ceiling in Western societies can be, and has been in many cases, shattered. In contrast, the glass ceiling in societies of the Near and Middle East is unique: it is bulletproof. The families who occupy the top level live in glorious luxury, protected in their palaces and limousines, behind bulletproof glass. Those who want to pass to the other side of the bulletproof glass ceiling have to join families "up above."

Nepotism is the Name of the Game

In the Islamic societies of the Near and Middle East, the most important characteristic of any individual is the family they are born in. Individuals do everything through family ties, and show loyalty first to family. All important decisions, including decisions concerning education, marriage, and work, are usually made through the family. Nepotism thrives at a very high level, starting from those with greatest power and influence.

Symbolic of the important role of the family is that Saudi Arabia, the oil-producing giant of the world (Russia, the United States, and Iran are in turn the next biggest oil producers), is the only state in the world that is named after a family, the House of Saud (established by Abdul Aziz ibn Abdul Rahman Al Saud, 1881–1953). The Crown Prince Abdullah continues as the de facto ruler of Saudi Arabia, since 1995 when his half-brother King Fahd suffered a stroke. The other Islamic states in the region also have governing elites that are characterized by family ties. In Morocco, King Mohammed VI succeeded his father King Hassan in 1999. In Jordan, King Abdolluh II succeeded his father King Hussein. In Syria, Bashar al-Assad "inherited" the Presidency from his father Hafez Assad in 2000.

From the perspective of prodemocracy advocates, perhaps the most painful continuation of "family rule" has been in Kuwait, the country "liberated" by the U.S.-led coalition in the first Gulf War of 1991. The "liberation" of Kuwait did lead to the expulsion of Saddam Hussein's Iraqi army from Kuwait, but it did not lead to any form of democracy or expanded freedoms. The Emir Sheik Jabir Ahmed Sabah was reinstalled as the ruler of Kuwait by the U.S.-led coalition and continues the complete power monopoly of the Sabah family.

For millions of people in the Middle East and around the world, the "liberation of Kuwait" is symbolic of what they see to be hypocritical American policies: preaching democracy and in practice supporting dictatorship. George Bush talks the talk on democracy, but he never walks the walk—so the critics around the world contend.

Unfortunately, "revolutionaries" and "nationalists" of the region have also ruled through family ties and seem to be continuing family dynasties, albeit under different names. For example, in 1969 the inept regime of King Idris in Libya was overthrown by "revolutionary" officers led by Captain Muammar Qadhafi. But the "democracy" discussed in Qadhafi's "Green Book" has not materialized, and it is Qadhafi's family who play the role of "people's representatives." Qadhafi's son Seif el-Islam el-Qadhafi is best positioned to take over from his father as the next Libyan strongman.

Egypt also seems to be held back from democracy by nepotism and a culture of "family first." The coup of 1952, eventually leading to the leadership of Gamal Abdel Nasser in 1954, meant that for the first time in two millennia Egypt was ruled by a native-born Egyptian. Nasser was succeeded by Anwar Sadat in 1970, who governed until his assassination in 1981, after which Hosni Mubarak took the reigns of command. During the over half century since the "nationalist" coup of Nasser and others, democratic opportunities have in many ways declined rather than increased in Egypt. For decades now, Hosni Mubarak has been repeatedly swept into power through "landslide" elections, the types associated with banana republics prior to the 1980s. The most "fast rising" political figure behind Hosni Mubarak is his son, Gamal Mubarak.

Fundamentalism, Democracy, and the "Good Copy Problem" in Islamic Societies

The so-called "spring" of democracy in the Islamic world since 2005 did bring some hints of potential reform and a possible weakening of family ties as the basis for power. Some of the changes that have been trumpeted as "democratic reform" certainly do hint at movement in the right direction. For example, in Egypt President Mubarak said in February 2005 that multiparty elections would be held for the post of President. In Bahrain, women were allowed to vote and run for office in parliamentary elections in 2002 (although no women won seats). In Kuwait there has been some indication that the ruling family may consider some weak forms of popular representation that include women. In Saudi Arabia, men over twenty-one years of age were allowed to vote for half of the places in local municipal elections, with the other half being appointed, in February, March, and April 2005. Of course, these elections represent symbolic changes at the local level, with real, national policymaking power remaining firmly in the hands of the Saudi family. Besides, the winners in these local Saudi elections proved to be Islamic fundamentalists on the so-called *Golden List* supported by hard-line conservatives.

Why did Islamic fundamentalists win the local Saudi elections in 2005? Why did Islamic fundamentalists manage to lead the fight against the Shah and take over the 1978–1979 revolution in Iran? Why have Islamic groups guided by Ayatollah Sistani and other leading clerics done so well in elections in at least Shi'a regions of Iraq? Why have Islamic parties done so well when democratic elections have been held, such as in Algeria in the late 1980s?

I believe the root reason is related to the good copy problem. The liberal professors, doctors, lawyers, and other professionals who represent the secular face of democracy are often a pale imitation, at best a "good copy," of Western models. To the masses in Islamic societies, these liberals lack authenticity. This is in part because local dictators have not allowed secular opposition groups to become openly active and to develop indigenous identities.

Movement toward an open society in the Near and Middle East seems to be according to the old saying: one step forward, two steps back. Nowhere is this more apparent than in Pakistan, which came into being as an Islamic Republic in 1956. The initial democratic promise of Pakistan was stunted by a coup that brought General Mohammed Ayub Khan to power in 1958. Ayub Khan was overthrown in 1969 by General Yahya Khan, and a popular uprising forced the government to hold elections. The army did not like the results of the elections and tried to suppress the outcome, resulting in civil war and the establishment of the breakaway state of Bangladesh in 1971. Thus, the "democracy" movement had first resulted in the breaking away of Pakistan from India in 1956, and then the breaking away of Bangladesh from Pakistan in 1971. Since then, each time a civilian government comes to power in Pakistan and there is a serious threat to the power of the military, a coup takes place and the head of the military reasserts a dictatorship. The twenty-first century has begun with a military junta headed by General Mosharaf.

One step backward, two steps forward also seems to be prevailing in Iran, particularly since the 1953 CIA-engineered coup against the democratically elected government of Mohammed Mossadegh. From 1953 to 1978, the ruling Shah allowed for some symbolic elections at local and national levels, but the *Majlis* (parliament) remained utterly powerless and the Shah remained an absolute (and isolated) ruler. Since 1979, elections for a *Majlis* and for the President of the Islamic Republic have been held regularly, but the constitution of Iran renders such elections meaningless. All laws and regulations endorsed by the *Majlis* and the government are vetted by an appointed *Council of Guardians*, consisting of Islamic fundamentalists. Most importantly, every institution, every official, every regulation, and every law is under the complete control of a "supreme leader," *marja-i-taqlid*, who is literally supposed to serve as a "source of imitation" for the nation.

The word of the supreme leader in Iran is more than a command, it is a commandment. Anyone who disobeys faces the ultimate punishment. In this way, as one critic noted, the revolution in Iran replaced "the turban for the crown," and the "thousand families" who ruled in the time of the Shah have simply been replaced by a thousand families who are intimately connected with the ruling mullahs.

Why Must the Bulletproof Glass Ceiling Be Removed?

Over 2,500 years ago, Plato pointed out in his timeless treatise *The Republic* why it is essential to remove all barriers to the social mobility of individuals. Addressing the members of an imaginary ideal society, Plato wrote:

> "You are, all of you in this community, brothers. But when god fashioned you, he added gold in the composition of those of you who are qualified to be Rulers ... silver in the Auxiliaries, and iron and bronze in the farmers and other workers. Now since you are all of the same stock, though your children will commonly resemble their parents, occasionally a silver child will be born of golden parents, or a golden child of silver parents, and so on. Therefore the first and most important of god's commandments to the Rulers is that in the exercise of their functions as Guardians their principal care must be to watch the mixture of metals in the character of their children. If one of their own children has traces of bronze or iron in its make-up, they must harden their hearts, assign it its proper value, and degrade it to the ranks of the industrial and agricultural class where it properly belongs: similarly, if a child of this class is born with gold or silver in its nature, they will promote it appropriately to be a Guardian or Auxiliary. And this they must do because there is a prophecy that the State will be ruined when it has Guardians of silver and bronze."[19]

The "prophecy" that the state will be ruined if it is not open to circulation of individuals, more talented persons moving up and less talented ones moving down, is repeated in different ways by many different thinkers since the time of the ancient Greeks. Modern researchers have discussed more specifically how the state will come to ruin under circumstances when circulation is not open. The basic argument is that disgruntled and motivated members of the nonelite, those stuck below the glass ceiling, will try to move up and bang their heads against barriers in frustration. After repeated but failed attempts to break through, the disgruntled nonelite will search for other, sometimes illegal ways, to improve their personal situation.

Closed systems are inefficient, particularly when they are kept in place by brute force. Even though the dictatorships of the Near and Middle East are floating on oceans of oil, the lack of open competition and circulation in these societies breed corruption and inefficiency. In this context, it should not be surprising that many people, particularly the young, experience a strong sense of injustice and despair.

AM I BEING TREATED FAIRLY?

The scene is a familiar one to all parents and caretakers of young children: a child runs over to complain: "That's not fair!" The complaint is often followed up with cries like: "It's my turn! She won't let me have my turn!" or "I want to take a turn, but he won't let me!"

Children learn to complain about what they see to be unfair treatment very early in their development. Cries of "Not fair!" are common among kindergartners. By the time individuals have grown up to become adults, the role of perceived fairness plays an even more central role in their lives. The concern with fairness is universal, and not just restricted to people living in democracies.

To understand the central role of fairness in our lives, we need to look back to our evolutionary past. A sense of fairness is not unique to humans, but is shared by some "lower" animals. Ethologists and biologists have shown that some animals have a sense of fair play, and react negatively when they are treated unfairly.[20] Monkeys become upset when others monkeys receive better rewards for the same work, or get rewards for doing no work at all. Animals have been shown to help one another to receive a "deserved" reward.

This is not to suggest that there is a "fairness gene" of some kind. The results of the Human Genome Project clearly show the inaccuracy of that kind of idea. Humans have far fewer genes than we had expected (something like 25,000 thousand), and only a few hundred genes are unique to humans. If there is a relationship between genetics and a sense of fairness, it comes about indirectly and through a very complex interaction between genes, and between genes and the environment.

The evolutionary roots of morality are behavioral and later cultural. Recent research is showing that culture is not unique to humans, and that some other "lower" animals pass on cultural characteristics across generations. For example, studies on chimpanzees and orangutans in the wild have shown patterns of socially transmitted behavior across generations. Such behavior includes group-specific styles of hunting for food, as well as vocal communications.[21] Put simply, groups of chimps and orangutans have been found to have their own ways of getting food and communicating with one another. These "cultural" characteristics are less similar to groups who live a greater distance away, suggesting that for chimps and orangutans contact with other groups of chimps and orangutans leads to more similarity in culture.

The functional approach to fairness, supported by empirical ethological research, also received support from some legal experts. For example, Alan Dershowitz argues that human rights have evolved from human experiences with "wrongs."[22] It is when humans have had terrible experiences, such as slavery and imprisonment for political activity, that the need for rights is recognized and eventually fulfilled.

Turn-Taking and Fairness

The evolutionary root of a sense of fairness is also behavioral and later cultural. A first step in this evolution is the emergence of functional behaviors that improve the survival chances of an animal. Take the example of the child who runs up to complain: "Its not fair, I want my turn!" The child is using a label, "my turn," to describe a behavior that is common to the lives of humans and many animals and has a long evolutionary history: turn-taking.

The behavior of turn taking must have emerged very early in the evolutionary history of social animals. In any animal group, turn-taking practices must be present for the group to have high survival possibilities. At the most primitive level, the practice could involve the strongest members of a group being the first to take a turn to eat, and the weakest being the last to eat. This would be the practice in a pride of lions, for example. There are also other, perhaps more communal examples: consider social life in a troop of monkeys. Turn taking and reciprocity in grooming one another is an essential part of group life.

The adaptive advantage of turn taking becomes clear when we consider what would happen if turn-taking is not practiced. For example, if turn-taking is not practiced in communications, then everyone is making noises and gestures at the same time and communication breaks down (which is the case in some dysfunctional families, both human and animal!). Imagine if turn-taking is not practiced at a road junction. Cars would be tangled up in traffic for days (and not just hours, the way it is in Los Angeles today). Or, consider if lawyers in court refused to take turns cross-examining witnesses; the courtroom would resemble a wrestling ring with no referee. Turn taking helps to smooth out human interactions and minimize conflict by creating expectations of correct behavior: individuals give others a turn because they know that they will have their turn.

Turn taking was central to the rituals that early humans developed in order to be able to live cooperatively in groups. Through turn taking, within group aggression can be minimized. Consider two very different rituals practiced by two groups living on different continents, the first group very high and the other very low on aggressivity. The Yanomamo Indians of Venezuela and Brazil are among the most aggressive people in the world. Their aggression is particularly targeted against rival groups. One way in which they control aggression within their own group is to practice turn-taking, even during "conflict" activities such as a chest-pounding contest:

> "Two men ... would step into the center. One would step up, spread his legs apart, bare his chest, and hold his arms behind his back, daring the other to hit him. The opponent would size him up, adjust the man's chest or arms so as to give himself the greatest advantage when he struck, and then step back to deliver his close-fisted blow. He would then wind up like a baseball pitcher, but keeping both feet on the ground, and deliver a tremendous wallop, with his fist to the man's left pectoral muscle ... The recipient would stand poised and take as many as four blows before demanding to hit his adversary."[23]

In this way, the two Yanomamo opponents take turns at chest-pounding, each being allowed to hit the other in turn as many times as he had been hit himself.

The Tiwi of North Australia are very different in that they are renowned for their peaceful ways.[24] They lived for centuries in isolation on Melville and Bathurst Islands and some of their unique customs survived well into the twentieth century, when the influence of Western colonists increased dramatically. One such traditional custom was for old men to have multiple wives, some of them very young girls, and for young men to not have a wife or to have a wife much older than himself. As men got older and gained resources and status, they acquired additional and younger wives. Combine this with the Tiwi traditional belief that women get pregnant through the work of spirits, and the situation is ripe for affairs between young men (typically without a wife) and young women (typically married to a much, much older man).

Not surprisingly, disputes in traditional Tiwi society typically involve an older man accusing a younger man of trying to seduce his wife (presumably, some young men did succeed in their attempts at seduction and served the role of "spirits" who make women pregnant). The accuser would confront the young man in a public place and loudly declare his complaints for all to hear, attracting more and more people to witness the ritual that was about to unfold. After some time spent with the older man haranguing the younger, declaring to all the world how ungrateful, deceitful, and rebellious the younger man had become, the two would take up positions some distance from one another, rather like a pitcher and a hitter in baseball. The older man would be armed with spears, but the younger man would be unarmed and would have to rely on his agility to dodge the spears thrown by the older man, while all the time remaining within the bounds of an invisible circle.

Why would the younger man simply not run away? Because if he did, the gathered crowd would drag him back: this is his day in "court," his turn to face his accuser, and he must keep dodging the thrown spears until one of the spears finally hits him and draws blood. The younger man can play to the crowd and use his greater agility to make the older man keep missing his target, but this must not go on for too long, or else the crowd will turn against the younger man. Once a spear has injured the younger man, the older man has had his turn and his day "in court," and the ritual is over.

Turn Taking: Rights and Duties

Turn taking evolved early in human evolutionary history, and much later became interpreted as involving rights and duties. How a turn is defined as a right or a duty depends on culture. For example, for a male member of the Yanomamo tribe, being hit in a chest-pounding duel gives you the right to have a turn at hitting your opponent; thus the opponent has a reciprocal duty of standing still to take your punch. For Tiwi men involved in a dispute, the accuser has a right to a turn to throw spears and the accused has a duty to just jump around "on the same spot" until he is hit and suffers an injury. Just as members of traditional societies have been socialized to understanding turn-taking rights and duties in particular ways, they are now being influenced to see rights and duties in alternative ways.

Rapidly expanding communication and transportation systems are exposing people in non-Western societies to rights and duties as interpreted in the West. In the case of the Tiwi and the Yanomamo, the first exposures came through contact with missionaries and traders, and later social science researchers and journalists. New, Western ideas about rights and duties emerged in these and other traditional societies around the world. An outcome has been the decline or even abandonment of many traditional practices, such as the Tiwi system of old men having multiple young wives and young men having no wives, and the Yanomamo practice of chest pounding.

The decline of traditional interpretations of rights and duties has been associated with the rise of awareness of new interpretations of rights and duties, particularly influenced by the West. No matter how much authorities in countries such as Saudi Arabia, Iran, and Egypt try, they are not able to prevent international media, communications systems (including e-mail and telephone), and transportation networks from influencing their citizens. Muslims and others in the Near and Middle East are witnessing the greater range of options enjoyed by people in the West, and this is influencing how they think about their own rights and duties. Hearing about and watching other people speak freely can lead us to think that we should have the same right.

I am not here using the term "rights" in a high-flown, abstract sense, but in a practical, everyday sense. That is, rights as involving increased choices in everyday life.[25] The key issue here is not even increases in material resources or poverty reduction in objective terms, but increases in the choices that people have available to them in important areas of life. More money can lead people to feel they have greater choices, but it need not. More money can lead to more options in consumer products, but might not lead to greater choices in the political arena. Revenue from oil has dramatically increased choices in the consumer market for many people in the Muslim world, but done nothing to increase their choices in the political sphere.

In Islamic societies of the Near and Middle East, you can be a millionaire, but you still will not have the right to free speech. You can have the money to own a fleet of luxury cars, but not have the freedom to go where you want, or even to drive a car (as is the case for women in some regions).

Besides, we now know that increased consumer choices without increased political awareness and participation is eventually likely to decrease our range of options. When freedom and choice is only available through consumerism, so that people have the freedom to buy more and more consumer goods but no corresponding political freedoms, this short-term abundance of consumer choices will very likely lead to lowered choices in the longer term as environmental pollution continues and resources are depleted.

The full range of choices available to us today will not be there if air and water pollution has increased and reserves of oil and other natural resources are at an end.[26]

Islamic Fundamentalists Feel the Heat

The images of political and cultural freedom beamed out by ever-expanding international media have also impacted on Islamic fundamentalists—who now feel more threatened than ever. Islamic fundamentalists are particularly incensed by two aspects of the images beamed out by democratic societies: equality for women and democratic decision making for everyone.

Since the advent of organized religion, traditionalist males have used the power of religion to maintain the dominance of men over women. This claim is not new, nor should it be controversial. The *Bible*, the *Torah*, and the *Koran* continue to be interpreted by traditionalists in ways that support the subordinate position of women, denying them important rights, including the right to join the clergy and become partners in the ongoing task of interpreting holy books. Just as the Pope is against the idea of women priests, so too are traditionalist Jewish and Islamic religious leaders against the idea of women rabbis and mullahs. But outside religious organizations, women have achieved equality "on the books" in Western societies, and they are pushing for greater equality in most non-Western societies, including in the Islamic world. Images of Western women enjoying political and social freedoms beamed out through film, music, radio, print, and other avenues worry Islamic traditionalists.

Traditionalist Muslim men fear that globalization will bring about changes in gender relations in the Islamic world, and they are adamant that women will not achieve equal rights in Islamic societies. Thus, religion is used again and again to justify the third-class status of women in the Near and Middle East. The rhetoric used by traditionalists involves variations of the "separate but equal," or "men and women are like two wings of a bird," arguments: men and women both have important roles to play, but these roles are very different from one another. Women are highly valued in *their* role, and men are highly valued in *their* different role, but the essential point to maintain is that these are different roles. Traditionalists argue that it is not a matter of "superior" and "inferior" roles, but simply different roles (unfortunately, history has numerous such examples of "separate but equal" arguments being used to support inequalities). Liberal interpretations of the *Koran* are wrong, according to traditionalists, because they try to wash away natural gender differences in the name of equal rights for women. The most powerful weapon in the hands of traditionalists for subjugating women is not throwing acid in the faces of disobedient women or even killing them, as has happened in some instances, but stirring up feelings of insecurity among large numbers of Muslim men. To understand this psychological process, we need to first consider gender roles and stereotypes in the Near and Middle East. This is an area of the world where the virginity of brides is sacred and honor killings continue to be practiced. "Good" women are those who do not have premarital sex, and once a woman is discovered to have had premarital sex she is automatically placed in the category of "bad" women.

Men, on the other hand, are not stereotyped as "bad" if they have premarital sex. Indeed, it is seen as "natural" for a man to be sexually active earlier and more often than women: there is no numerical limit to the number of "temporary" wives Shi'a men can have in addition to the four "permanent" wives all Muslim men are permitted. This is an extreme version of the well known "double standard" applied to men and women until very recently in Western societies (like most social practices, this "double standard" is fading away gradually rather than disappearing suddenly, so it still has some influence in Western societies).

But men also have sexual relationships outside marriage, and the puzzle is who are the women they have sex with? Clearly, from the logic of the dominant culture it must be "bad women." Thus men in the near and Middle East see the world of women as divided, with a huge unbridgeable gulf between the two groups. On the one side are the "good" women, who include their mothers, sisters, daughters, cousins, and potential and actual wives; and on the other side are ruined women, damned women, and the women who sleep with men outside marriage. Traditionalists play on fears among Muslim men that globalization and "progressive values" may lead Muslim wives, daughters, mothers, sisters, or other relatives to move from the category of "good" to "bad" women. Along with this, traditionalists raise fears that Muslim men will lose the reigns of control in their own homes, and that wives and daughters will disobey the "man of the house."

EXITING THE FIRST FLOOR

The first floor changes the identities of some individuals in such a way that they feel they have no voice in decisions that impact their lives, and they have no way of improving their situation by taking individual action. These perceptions are associated with increasingly intense feelings of shame and anger.

The most salient emotional experience of Islamic communities over the last few decades has been feelings of collective shame. This is symbolized by the failure to establish a free and independent Palestine, and the "temporary" presence of American agents in the most holy lands of Islam: Saudi Arabia, housing Mecca and Medina, holy sites for all Muslims; Iraq, housing Najaf and Karbela, holy sites particularly for Shi'a Muslims. As bin Laden and other terrorist leaders have repeatedly reminded the world, American-backed dictators continue to rule over most Muslim people.

The shame associated with collective failure is mirrored by shame arising out of individual ineptitude and ineffectiveness: many Muslims feel they have no voice, no control over events that impact them daily, and no merit-based opportunities in their own societies. Decision making and opportunities are monopolized by a small, dictatorial minority. These widespread experiences lead some individuals to climb further up the staircase to terrorism.

CHAPTER 6

Second Floor: Those Americans Are to Blame!

BEAR AND PORCUPINE FOREIGN POLICIES

When it comes to the foreign policy of a world power toward weaker nations, such as that of the United States toward Jordan Saudi Arabia, Iran, and other such third world states, there are two extremes: the "bear" and the "porcupine" policies. These policies have different implications for the identity of the populations of weaker nations.

The bear policy involves the greater power enveloping the smaller state in a tight embrace, a bear hug, so that the smaller state almost becomes invisible: its indigenous identity becoming submerged.

As the enormous bear wraps its arms around and smothers the smaller creature, it almost looks as if the bear intends to swallow up what it embraces. The little creature being embraced feels suffocated, overwhelmed, and in grave danger. In desperation, the crushed little creature tries to prod, pinch, kick, punch, and even tickle the great bear in an effort to make it let go.

But the bear gets annoyed by the struggles of the little creature in its embrace; it can't understand why anyone would *not* want to be embraced by it. After all, the bear is all-powerful and can protect smaller creatures. Also, those embraced take on the smell of the bear, and get lost in its thick fur; they become more like a bear in some ways, and surely that can only be a good thing, from the bear's point of view.

The trouble with the bear hug is that at least some of those creatures being embraced become unhappy in the tight grip of the huge bear. They

want to enjoy the freedom to find their own path in the woods, to develop their own identity, even though it may involve danger and possible
attacks from other animals. They call out to the bear and demand to
be let go, but the bear is too busy enjoying the embrace. The bear has
its nose up in the air and is looking around, seeking honey and other
treats.

Sometimes powerful nations take a very different approach to dealing
with smaller states; instead of embracing the smaller states as tightly as
possible, they try to control them by acting like a giant porcupine. The
very long, sharp quills of the giant porcupine keep the smaller creatures
at a distance, and preferably boxed up in a corner, isolated, and unable to
develop their identities through contact with others. Each time a small
creature tries to break out of isolation, hundreds of formidable sharp
quills force it back into a corner.

Being kept at a distance from the giant porcupine has advantages and
disadvantages for a smaller creature. One advantage is that a smaller
creature can at least be seen, and it might find a little room to move
about in its corner, despite its discomforts, and show itself for what it
really is. When it is looked at, it is clearly recognized as separate and
independent. The small creature calls out to the world: "Here I am, true
to myself, you too can be true to yourselves. Come and join me in the
struggle for freedom against the satanic porcupine!"

But a huge disadvantage for the small creature is that it is excluded,
segregated, and not allowed to move about or develop freely. Not surprisingly, the cornered, isolated little creature often becomes bitter, frustrated, and potentially aggressive.

The United States has acted as a porcupine with a number of countries,
particularly Cuba, Iran, Syria, and North Korea. The United States has
placed trade embargoes and tight travel restrictions on these countries,
and made every attempt to isolate them diplomatically. This is the case
of the giant porcupine using long, sharp quills to force smaller creatures
into a corner.

A problem with the porcupine foreign policy is that a country that is
isolated may become a client of a large country that is an economic and/or
political rival. For example, Iran has developed closer ties with Russia,
China and India, and thus the United States has been replaced as the chief
supplier of arms and many other materials to Iran. Similarly, Venezuela,
Brazil, and other Latin American countries (e.g., Bolivia) are starting to
purchase more military hardware from non-U.S. sources. Also, when a
number of smaller countries are placed into a corner, they may break
out of their isolation by banding together. For example, at the dawn of
the twenty-first century Cuba has developed closer ties with Venezuela,
Iran, Brazil, and a number of other countries with governments opposed
by U.S. administrations.

Small countries pushed into isolation have all the excuses in the world to be despotic internally, and aggressive externally. Aggressive dictators thrive in this kind of situation, and they use the threat of the "enemy at the gates" to crush all internal debate and opposition. Aggression on the part of the United States, the "great enemy at the gates," is an important factor keeping dictatorships in power in Cuba, Iran, North Korea, Syria, and now Venezuela—a country that is slipping into dictatorship.

A porcupine foreign policy can work in some cases. For example, Libya's abandonment of its program for weapons of mass destruction and the avowed end to its support for terrorism has been interpreted as an outcome of Western economic sanctions and pressure from Washington. However, this is a rare success for the porcupine foreign policy. A better approach, prevailing wisdom claims, is to go to the other extreme and bear hug these countries.

And so the United States has clung to a bear-hug policy, embracing countries such as Saudi Arabia, Egypt, and Pakistan so tightly that the inhabitants of those countries inevitably blame America for everything that they see is wrong with the world. After all, when you are in the grip of a huge bear, what else can you see?

Blaming the Bear

The medical doctor, the street vendor, the home maker, the school teacher, the widower, the university student, the illiterate villager, the teenage schoolgirl, the farmer, the journalist, the preacher, and the singer ... Tens of millions of people in the Near and Middle East are utterly discontented with their identities, their societies, and with their personal situations. It is impossible to exaggerate the red-hot frustration and fuming anger experienced by most of these people, particularly over the last half century. Their societies are going through convulsive changes but never meeting expectations, and their governments seem utterly incapable of managing changes effectively. Most obviously, their governments show themselves to be completely disconnected from the everyday experiences of the masses.

But how is it that governments in the Near and Middle East continue to survive even though they are so far removed from the majority of the population. Should there not be a collapse of government? Should the basic mechanisms to keep order not stop functioning? Why do the deep frustrations of the majority of the people not impact on "their" governments? Why is it that so much anger and hatred is instead directed at America, vilified as the "Great Satan," and against Israel, the so-called "Little Satan"? By answering these questions, we can better explain the thoughts and actions of people who reach the second floor of the staircase to terrorism.

We shall see that there are two main mechanisms that serve the continuation of dictatorships in the region. The first has to do with the paradoxical effect of oil, the second concerns displacing or "redirecting" negative feelings onto outsiders. Both of these are important in shaping events on the second floor. The "paradox of oil" allows dictatorships in oil-producing nations to act independently from the populations of their own societies, while "displacement" allows these dictatorships to turn criticism away from themselves and onto "external enemies."

AN IMAGINED COUNTRY AND THE OIL PARADOX

Imagine you become a citizen of a new country, one that would be built completely from scratch. There are as yet no political or social traditions or institutions in this country, although for the time being there is a ruling group, acting as a kind of "caretaker" government. But the opportunity exists for you to build your Utopia, the ideal society from your point of view.

You have the opportunity to choose some of the characteristics of your new country. One of your choices concerns resources: do you want your country to have huge oil reserves? Imagine what an enormous advantage having oil reserves could give you, black gold oozing out of the ground— easy money. Think about the many uses to which oil money could be put. Education, health, pensions, hospitals, roads, and bridges ... the list is endless. How can huge oil reserves be wrong for your future Utopia?

But if your immediate reaction is to say "Yes to huge oil reserves!" you could be making an enormous mistake, because you may be opening up the possibility that your country will experience the *oil paradox*, wealth from oil sustains poverty among the majority of the population. Instead of becoming affluent, the majority remains poor. Of the thirty-four less-developed countries that have significant oil and natural gas resources, up to half of the population in twelve of these countries live on less than $1 a day.

The oil paradox that plagues the oil rich nations of the world is also characterized by enormous rifts between the government and the majority of the people. About two-thirds of the thirty-four less-developed countries that have significant oil and gas reserves also have undemocratic governments, some of which are among the most brutal dictatorships in the world.

To better understand the oil paradox, think back to your imagined society, which has not yet developed political traditions and institutions. Together with other individual members of your new society, you are interested to build a democracy. You attempt to engage the (temporary) government in dialogue. But if the government already has high revenues from the sale of oil, it can act independent from the people.

In effect, income from oil reserves means that there is no necessity for the government to tax citizens or depend on them in other important ways. Actually, the government will not even need to have a dialogue with the people. In effect, oil revenues give the government the power to ignore the people. Instead of serving as a "temporary government," the ruling elite in our imagined country can now develop strong ties to foreign powers, build up the military and internal security agencies, and achieve an unassailable power base. In other words, the ruling elite can become like the Saudi regime or any of the other dictatorships in the Near and Middle East region.

The idea of an "oil paradox" is not new and is well known in oil producing societies. I first learned about it in the early 1970s when I was visiting Tehran during the boom years, and one of my relatives told me about his salary for a "thirteenth month" of work for the government of the Shah. When I asked him to explain how anyone could receive money for a thirteenth month, given that there are only twelve months in each year, he said, "Oil money means the Shah does not need us, the people, but he gives us special treats just to act like good children and keep quiet." But by the late 1970s, oil "bribery" money was not enough to keep up with rapidly rising expectations among the fast growing Iranian population (the population of Iran just about doubled in the two decades before the revolution, and doubled again during the two decades after the revolution). The Shah attempted to compensate the shortfall in government revenue by raising taxes, but this actually made him more vulnerable to pressures from the people.

How long can the dictatorships of the Near and Middle East continue? One answer is that they can continue as long as the oil reserves last. With oil revenues at their disposal, the local dictators can support huge security systems to stifle dissent at home, and gain the support of foreign powers by assuring stability and payment for lucrative arms sales and other imports.

In essence, the dictators of the Near and Middle East use oil revenues to bribe two sets of people. First, they bribe people within their own countries, particularly military and security forces, to keep order and prevent the overthrow of their regime. Second, they bribe international corporations by buying huge amounts of "needed" products, particularly expensive military hardware, and the international corporations in turn persuade various governments, including the major powers, to support the dictatorships.

But this picture of how oil-based dictatorships survive is too limited, because although it includes *rational* aspects of behavior, what people are consciously aware of, it does not include the *irrational*, the thoughts and actions that remain outside awareness. I describe the oil paradox as being part of the rational world, because it arises from the actual rather than imagined monopoly that dictators have over oil resources, and the actual rather than assumed distance that dictators can maintain between themselves and the rest of the population using revenue from oil sales. But the oil paradox can also be interpreted as part of a broader picture of an irrational human world.

Our Irrationality, Yet Again

Sigmund Freud is so far the only genius to have developed his talents in the field of psychology, and his greatest contribution is that he helped us see our own irrationality, at both the individual and collective levels. Freud leads us to recognize that at least in some situations we really are not aware of what we are doing, and we are even less aware of why we are doing what we do (of course, most of us are all too ready to accept this as true about others, but not about ourselves). We fight wars, make peace, fall in and out of love, abandon plans, suddenly recall incidents from years ago, forget important dates, set unachievable goals for our ourselves, 'accidentally' divulge secrets and insult others through slips of the tongue, and in countless other ways reveal our irrational nature.

This does not mean that we are incapable of rationalizing; indeed, we are extremely creative and effective in coming up with explanations that seem to justify our actions as rational. The father who beats his child mercilessly explains that "it's a jungle out there and the beatings will help the kid toughen up to face the real world." The bigot who discriminates against minorities explains that "they are out to get us, so we had better get them first." The politician who plunges his country into war, resulting in thousands of deaths and the destruction of entire cities, rationalizes by claiming that "we have no choice but to wage war for the sake of peace and democracy." Such rationalizations do not mean that we acted in a rational way in the first place, but they do effectively lead us to neglect the real, irrational reasons for the way we behave, in war and in peace.

Behavior on the second floor of the staircase to terrorism is in major ways irrational, and this is particularly because of the way dictators direct the attention of people in their societies.

HATING THE "GREAT SATAN" AND THE "LITTLE SATAN": THE DISPLACEMENT OF AGGRESSION

If Israel did not exist, the dictators of the Near and Middle East would no doubt invent an Israel, an external enemy, an "easy target" onto which they could redirect the negative energies boiling over in their own closed, despotic societies. The reality of Israel has helped oil-based dictatorships to survive, and to understand how this came about we must explore the roots of *displaced aggression*, action intended to harm others by a person who feels provoked against a third-party target who is not responsible for the provocation.

The idea of displaced aggression was formalized in the writing of Sigmund Freud, who considered displaced aggression in both interpersonal and intergroup relations. Sam has had a very difficult day at work, and an even worse time in traffic on the way home. By the time Sam reaches home and walks through the front door, everything in the world seems to be wrong and she lashes out at the first person who crosses her path, her ten-year-old daughter. Sam hits the girl and confines her to the basement of the house for the rest of the evening "because that girl's acting stupid again!" This is an example of displaced aggression at the interpersonal level, Sam displacing aggression onto her daughter— unfortunately not an uncommon behavior pattern for aggressive parents like Sam, and one which their daughters are likely to pass on to the next generation.

Displacement of aggression is perhaps just as common at the inter-group level. The members of religious group X are "divinely inspired" by the conviction that their way of thinking and their way of doing things "follows God's commands," and that the members of other religious faiths are, at best, misguided. When the economy declines, or a natural disaster strikes, or the level of crime increases, or government programs fail, or other nations are making faster progress, or women and other minorities gain equal rights, or whatever else happens to make the members of religious group X feel discontented with the present state of the world, they vent their frustrations by vehemently attacking the members of other religious faiths. "Those heathen" should open their eyes and convert to the right path, because they are knowingly or unknowingly doing Satan's work! We have to change them in order to save the world! And if they won't change their ways, then life must be made difficult for them."

Displaced aggression is irrational, because the aggressors are not aware of the real reasons why they are attacking a third party. Sam is not aware that frustrations arising out of her job situation and her relationships with her boss, who is too powerful for her to attack directly, are the real reasons she hit her daughter, who is too small and weak to hit her back. The members of religious group X are not aware that it is their frustrations with forces too large for them to control, such as competition from foreign powers or world economic trends, that lead them to attack the members of other faiths.

The Roots of Displaced Aggression

The roots of displaced aggression are pent up feelings of frustration, dissatisfaction, and anger that evolve in all human relationships. Even the closest of ties, between lovers, between parents and children, between siblings, between colleagues at work, and between best friends, all human relationships are associated with both negative and positive feelings (recall our discussion of Freud's psychology in Chapter 2). Even adoring couples have to take care to prevent their negative feelings from rising to the surface and overpowering their relationships; just a slip of the tongue, or a birthday or wedding anniversary forgotten, can intentionally or unintentionally result in an emotional explosion and angry fights. Suddenly, lovers can find themselves hating their partners and shouting cruel words at one another.

The man who lovingly brought red roses home for his beloved wife ends up throwing the roses on the floor in a rage, and the wife who kissed and thanked her husband for the roses now slams the door in his face and shouts at him to "Go away!" When they succeed in maintaining close relationships, it is through managing their sometimes intense negative feelings toward one another. Part of this "management" involves redirecting or "displacing" negative feelings to others outside their relationship.

The loving couple make private jokes about their friends and develop similar views about what is hateful about the world, from "terrible" fashion trends to "boring" people they know. Family members construct their own subculture, sharing preferences, biases, and private nicknames and jokes that keep outsiders mystified. Each case of failure experienced by the lovers, or the family members, leads to some outside cause being blamed for their problems.

At the intergroup level, also, displacement plays a vital role in maintaining positive relations internally. However, in the group context an important difference is that there is a leader directing feelings, actions, and thoughts. The role of the leader is particularly important in large complex societies, both in dictatorships and in democracies. Group members identify with the group through the leader, who at the national level has tended to be male (rather like the father figure in a traditional family). The group leader directs all negative feelings inside the group onto particular targets outside the group. Consider, for example, the case of the church leader who directs everyone in his church to love one another like brothers and sisters, but to treat as "misguided," or "sinful," or even "devilish," the members of other churches. Just as Ayatollah Khomeini and some other Muslim leaders have blasted the United States as being "The Great Satan," some evangelical Christian leaders in the United States have labeled the founder of Islam as a "demon-possessed pedophile."[27]

Both Sides Say: "You Are Either with Us or against Us"

President George W. Bush's statements to the effect that: "You are either with us or against us," played an important role in displacing aggression after the tragedy of September 11. The first effect of his speeches was to divide the world and to make a sharp distinction between the ingroup, "us, the good guys" and "them, the bad guys." In the Bush picture of the world, there are no fuzzy boundaries, no uncertainties as to who belongs to which group, and how each group should be labeled. It is like watching an old fashioned Hollywood cowboy and Indian movie, where the cowboys inside the circled wagons are clearly "the good guys" and the Indians outside the circled wagons are clearly "the bad guys" and are going to get what they obviously deserve, what all bad guys deserve, a walloping.

The second effect of President Bush's "with us or against us" speeches was to increase pressure toward conformity and obedience within the United States. Those who are "with us" are the patriots, and those who are against us must be either part of the enemy or directly or indirectly aiding the enemy. Of course, this process of increased ingroup cohesion, conformity, and obedience as a result of external threat is not peculiar to Republican administrations and presidents. The same kind of "rallying around the flag" was evident during the Second World War when a Democrat, Franklin Roosevelt, was in the White House. The internment of Japanese Americans and the suppression of sentiments critical of government policies in news-papers, on campuses, and in society generally during World War Two reflected the same broad trend of increased conformity in the face of external threat, irrespective of which party is in power.

The increased ingroup conformity and obedience witnessed during times of intergroup conflict serves to suppress negative sentiments inside the group, but another strategy for coping with negative sentiments is displacement onto out-groups, those who do not belong on our side, who are not "with us," but are positioned as "against us." The leader plays a vital role in directing negative sentiments onto specific out-groups, typically those who are seen to be dissimilar to the ingroup. Thus, displacement of negative sentiments is not onto randomly selected targets, but targets that are dissimilar from the ingroup in specific ways that are argued to be important, such as religious affiliation, race, and nationality.

In terms of dissimilarity, the Muslims of the Near and Middle East make the near perfect target for American displacement of aggression. This target is weak, so it cannot retaliate on a large scale—terrorism is only small-scale war and its impact is more psychological than directly material. The number of Americans killed by terrorists in the last decade, including in the attacks of September 11, is far less than the number of

Americans killed in road accidents in the same period. Even though the number of homicides in America declined in the early years of the new millennium to levels not seen since the mid-1960s and late 1970s, in an average year the number of Americans killed by terrorists is far fewer than the number killed in violent crime incidents. Thus, the threat posed by "Islamic terrorists" seems far larger than it really is, in part because such terrorists originate from a culture that is described, particularly by Evangelical Christians, as very distant from American culture.

Increasing activism by Christian groups, such as those who have vowed to "reclaim America for Christ," and the explicit invasion of religious values into political, educational, social, and other spheres in the United States through Mr. Bush and the new Republican leadership, has created an atmosphere in which Muslims are more clearly identified as a "dissimilar out-group." Of course, such an outcome will not have been intended by all of the Republican leadership.

Similarly, in maneuvering to displace negative feelings onto out-groups, dictators in oil-producing societies of the Near and Middle East may not all have intended to reinforce the "us versus them" picture of the world, but in effect that is what they have achieved. The United States is vilified to an extraordinary degree, even among many affluent Muslims who were educated in the United States.

Thus, displaced aggression has served the purposes of particular leaders in both the United States and in the Near and the Middle East. By maneuvering to displace negative feelings onto selected dissimilar out-groups, group leaders achieve at least four strategic goals. First, cohesion is increased within the ingroup and this makes it easier to mobilize group resources and energies. Second, displaced aggression heightens the danger from an external threat, and this makes it easier to pressurize and silence dissenters within the ingroup. Third, support for the leadership increases, as people "rally around the flag." Fourth, the leadership is pressured by the momentum of group member sentiments to adopt more aggressive postures, or otherwise move aside for more aggressive leadership.

EXITING THE SECOND FLOOR

The displacement of aggression is an effective strategy through which to maintain control at home, which is a lesson many group leaders learn. National leaders, irrespective of whether they are heads of dictatorships or democracies, find it highly useful to redirect negative feelings onto dissimilar outsiders. The presence of an external enemy can help to bolster internal support and make popular even the most unpopular leaders. Again and again, dictators in the Near and Middle East have found this to be an effective strategy.

Those who wonder why the clerics in Iran insist on whipping up anti-American sentiments and organizing and leading rallies against the United States on a regular basis should keep in mind that without the "Great Satan" to fight against, the regime in Tehran would collapse more quickly. Similarly, without Israel as a target of displaced aggression, the Arab dictatorships would disintegrate. This does not mean that there is no limit to the effectiveness of displaced aggression as a way of keeping control. There is a definite limit, and it is set in large part by the realities of the economic situation.

When the oil starts to dry up in the Near and Middle East, then governments will be forced on the one hand to cut spending on both imports and support for favored military and security groups, and on the other hand to increase taxation. When this happens, all hell will break loose. The loyalty of military and security forces, as well as foreign "allies" will be tested. Also, the people will want effective services and programs, as well as accountability, in lieu of the increasingly burdensome taxes they are paying. They will search for ways to put pressure on the government.

Another very important factor in this situation is rising aspirations: ever-expanding international media and communications systems are creating new and growing expectations. Even when oil prices reach $200 a barrel, oil revenues are not enough to meet the rising expectations of fast growing populations that have their eyes on the consumer life in San Francisco, London, and Paris.

In this context, individuals who develop a readiness to physically displace aggression, and actively seek out opportunities to do so, eventually leave the second floor and climb more steps, in search of ways to take action against the United States and its allies. Along this path, such individuals begin the process of becoming more deeply engaged in a morality that condones terrorism.

CHAPTER 7

Third Floor: The Ends Justify the Means

Mangled body parts scattered around the obliterated marketplace, a torn off arm dangling from the top of a partially destroyed wall; hair, and one side of a face stuck to a burned car hood, feet not matching but seemingly ready to walk detached from an upper body, intestines strewn along the blood covered pavement; skin, and flesh, and blood, pasted on the road, cries for help from people fortunate enough not to have been killed by the blast, the sound of police and ambulance sirens homing in on the scene of another devastating suicide bombing . . . those terrorists! Those inhumane creatures! Surely they have no morality.

Women, children, senior citizens, lovers taking a stroll, mothers proudly displaying their new babies, young men who recently became fathers . . . suicide bombers indiscriminately kill them all. They have no sense of shame, no sense of right and wrong, no sense of fairness, and no sense of morality. Such is our reaction to terrorists—we think they are divorced from morality, we see them as morally disengaged.

Both lay people and experts have tended to share this reaction. Unfortunately, this is a completely incorrect understanding of terrorism and morality. Terrorists have a very strong sense of right and wrong integrated in their identity, but it is not our sense of right and wrong; and they are highly committed to a morality that serves as the core of their identity, but it is not our morality. Indeed, it is because their morality is so integral to their identity, and serves as a solid foundation for their categorical ideas about right and wrong, about who is with them and who is against them, that they are able to commit terrorist acts.

The centrality of *their* morality to the identity of suicide bombers allows them to sidestep what the ethologist Konrad Lorenz termed the "inhibitory mechanisms" that make it difficult for one human to kill another.[28] An inhibitory mechanism comes into effect when one animal gives signals of submission, leading another animal to limit its aggression. Lorenz points out that inhibitory mechanisms serve to limit intraspecies aggression within many groups of animals. For example, when two wolves fight, after some initial aggression the weaker wolf will give signals of submission, and this will inhibit the stronger wolf from continuing the fighting to result in serious injury or death.

Inhibitory mechanisms serve a vital evolutionary purpose, in that they help to limit injury and death particularly to young males who could be the "prize fathers" of the next generation. The weaker wolf in a fight between two males today could be a young wolf who, if allowed to escape today's fight without serious injury, could become the champion male in the next few years. Thus, it is functional for inhibitory mechanisms to inhibit intraspecies aggression.

Human aggression can also be diminished by inhibitory mechanisms. Imagine trying to kill another person at close quarters. You would smell and feel the victim, and have to remain firm in the face of cries of appeal, sobs of despair, and pleading looks. Even if you are physically strong enough to complete the killing, you may not be able to overcome the inhibitory mechanisms that limit your aggression.

But there are ways in which you could sidestep inhibitory mechanisms. One way highlighted by Lorenz is the development of weapons that allow you to attack the target from a long distance away, thus preventing inhibitory mechanisms from coming into play. It is difficult to make pleading effective if the killer is attacking using a weapon that can kill from tens or hundreds of miles away. In such cases, it is impossible for the killer to hear, or see, or smell, or touch the victim, who may appear as just a dot on a radar screen. Although terrorists sometimes use distance as a means of sidestepping inhibitory mechanisms, they also use moral commitment as another means of nullifying the effect of inhibitory mechanisms so as to carry out acts of terrorism at close quarters.

The moral commitment of terrorists to their cause allows them to rigidly categorize the social world into "us" and "them," "friends" and "enemies." The out-group, "them," can include people actively engaged in the military and in police forces, but it can also include ordinary unarmed citizens, passersby on the street, or commuters on a train or bus. If these people are not actively resisting the government, then from the terrorists' point of view they are legitimate targets of aggression.

The moral commitment of terrorists allows them to sidestep the kinds of inhibitory mechanisms that would prevent you and I from seriously harming others. The out-group is categorized as different, as unclean, as corrupted, and ungodly. Terrorists believe that what they are doing will actually save the out-group from themselves and improve the world. These are part of the myths that support terrorism.

Terrorist Myths

In the process of becoming engaged with the morality of terrorism, terrorists also adopt *terrorist myths*, beliefs about the world that are wrong but nevertheless serve to justify the actions of terrorists according to their own moral system. Terrorist myths serve a similar purpose to rape myths, that justify rape in the mind of the rapist.[29] An example of a rape myth is the idea that victims secretly enjoy the experience of being raped, and when they say "No!" they really mean "Yes!" Terrorist myths are more complex, because they are about societies as well as about individual victims.

Terrorist myths share with rape myths the idea that the individual victims do not really know their own minds, and that they are somehow misunderstanding their own true desires and interests. But terrorist myths go further by assuming that people as a collectivity are living an illusion, and that as a group they need to "wake up" and see reality. For example, people need to see that the central government is not only corrupt but also weak and vulnerable enough to fall if put under enough pressure. Terrorist attacks are intended to highlight the vulnerability of authorities, so that people "take heart" and rebel. Even the Oklahoma City bombers held this myth, believing that their attack on a federal building could serve as a spark for a larger uprising against the federal government.

Terrorist myths have their own internal logic, centered on ideas about the functions served by acts of terror, the main ones being to:

- show that the authorities are weak and vulnerable to attacks;
- prove that the authorities are unable to control events;
- lower allegiance to the authority institutions;
- create a sense of instability and lawlessness in society;
- create a sense of helplessness among the population;
- give the impression of terrorist organizations as being very powerful, a force to be reckoned with;
- give the impression that there will be no end to terrorist acts until "final victory";
- support the illusion that the victims of terrorist acts have "died in a good cause."

Of course, from among all morally committed people, very few carry out terrorist acts. What is it about the morality of some individuals that allows them to become suicide bombers? We need to recognize that terrorists adhere strongly to a moral system that is very different from our own. We need to understand this different value system, and recognize that it arises under certain conditions—not because of the evil nature of an individual but because of the evil nature of the context in which an individual has grown up and lives in, as well as the nature of the identity demanded by the social context. This is a major challenge for us, to progress beyond our own ethnocentrism, to see the world from the point of view of others rather than ourselves, to recognize the terrorists' point of view.

But seeing the terrorists' point of view involves an even more profound shift, because it requires us to move out of the individualism that Western education has taught us. We have been trained to identify causes within individuals, to see the person as an independent entity, as "self contained." The ethos of self-help and individual responsibility colors and shapes our picture of the world.

But this picture of the "independent mind" does not help us to understand the terrorists' point of view. Instead, we need to see the *mind in culture*, and thoughts and ideas arising through culture. This shifts the emphasis from the individual's morality to the morality pervasive in a context, from the motives "self-contained individuals" are assumed to have for their identities to the social demands that society has for the identities of interdependent persons. The question is no longer: "Why does this person lack our morality?" but "What is the morality shared by the group in which this individual has been trained?" Instead of condemning individual terrorists for lacking a sense of right and wrong, we now look at the very different way in which right and wrong is seen by terrorist-producing cultures.

The "Normal" Person Becomes a Terrorist

The first and most important point to understand about terrorist-producing cultures is that they would lead many ordinary people to become transformed and to take on the identity of terrorists. Empirical research shows that this claim is not an exaggeration. Individuals with normal personality profiles, people like you and I, could be shaped to "become" terrorists in such cultures.

Of course, such a claim will immediately and vehemently be rejected by us, because we have been taught to believe in "individual responsibility," "self help," and "individual merit," and the idea that each person gets what she or he deserves in life, and can shape his or her life. If someone becomes a terrorist, according to this view, then it is because that person made himself or herself a terrorist. It is his or her personal responsibility, because each of us determines our own destiny. We are "self made."

The idea and practice of individual responsibility, and individualism generally, has shown some societal benefits in the context of Western countries such as the United States. After all, the American ideology of self-help and "you can make it if you try" is associated with hope and many successes, including among immigrants and minorities. The power of the American "self-help" ideology is undeniable. America is a strong magnet for millions around the world because it is seen as the land of opportunity, a place where "anybody can make it"—this simple idea conjures up an exciting and well known "rags to riches" image of an immigrant who just got off the last boat and is about to dive into the melting pot of New York City.

The power of the American dream testifies to the power of the context in shaping individual thoughts and actions. People who believe in the American Dream help to drive the motor of the U.S. economy. But just because people believe in the American Dream does not mean that all of the assumptions underlying this dream are correct. For example, the American Dream assumes that there is an exceptionally high level of social mobility, individuals moving up and down the social hierarchy, in the United States. This implies that a working class person is more likely to move up to the middle class in America than in other industrialized societies.

But the facts show otherwise: poor individuals are no more likely to move up the social hierarchy in the United States than they are in other Western societies.[30] Social mobility in the United States is only slightly higher than it is in England, stereotyped as "class based," and only slightly lower in the United States than in Sweden, stereotyped as "socialist." That means a working class person has a slightly lower chance of joining the middle class in England than in the United States, and a slightly higher chance of doing the same in Sweden than in the United States. But the actual differences are insignificant.

Related to this is the greater income disparity between the rich and the poor in the United States compared to other Western societies.[31] In the United States, about 30 percent of the share of income or consumption is by the rich (10 percent of the population), whereas in Sweden, Germany, and Japan it is about 22 percent, and in France and Canada about 25 percent. The share of income or consumption enjoyed by the poorest 20 percent of the population is about 5 percent in the United States, 9 percent in Sweden, Germany, and Japan, and about 7 percent in France and Canada. Despite this actual difference in income disparity in the United States, and despite social mobility being about the same in the United States as it is in other industrialized societies, the popular myth is that the United States is "the land of opportunity." This is an example of the dominant culture influencing individual perceptions, to some significant degree divorced from reality.

In the United States context, we can find important examples of "mind in culture," individual consciousness being shaped by the dominant ideology to arrive at a view of society that differs in important respects from the actual state of affairs. At one level, it is not important that society is not more open, or that income disparities are relatively high, because people are socialized to believe in the "rags to riches" American Dream. The context is larger than the individual; and this is a lesson we need to keep in mind as we consider the thoughts and actions of those who make their way up to the third floor of the staircase to terrorism.

By the time individuals climb up to the third floor of the staircase to terrorism, they are experiencing extremely high levels of frustration and have a strong sense of injustice. They see their societies as unjust, but have found no effective means of making their voices heard or participating in decision making. They feel shut out by those in power positions. When they look for ways of resolving their problems, for ways of improving the situation, their leaders guide them to look for foreign enemies. They come to believe that powerful enemies threaten their societies, their faith, and their families, and are the cause of their misfortunes. Their leaders identify the main enemy as the United States and Israel, in that order.

But how can anyone fight the United States, the sole superpower of the world? By what means?

BY ANY MEANS POSSIBLE

Do the ends justify the means? This is a broad question that often leads to the answer: "It depends on the ends." In some situations, it is argued, the ends do justify the means. Consequently, whatever one has to do to reach the ends is justified. For example, in order to defeat the Soviet Communist empire, some American government officials believe it was justified to support Islamic fundamentalists, including bin Laden and his associates, in the 1970s and 1980s. The resulting Taliban regime in Afghanistan was not good, but on the whole this support for Islamic fundamentalists was a justified means toward the larger goal of defeating Communism.

Similarly, some argue that continued American support for dictatorships in the Near and Middle East is necessary as a means of achieving a steady supply of relatively cheap oil. According to this logic, the alternative is much worse, because it would mean the long-term demise of the United States and victory for rivals such as China. World oil production has reached a peak in the first decade of the twenty-first century, and the United States can only remain the top world power if it takes bold steps to secure the control of oil supply. According to this reasoning, the "invasion" of Iraq is also justified, because it has given American oil companies easier access to one of the largest oil and gas reserves remaining in the world. According to the same logic, the tens of thousands of people killed and the hundreds of thousands seriously injured during and since the invasion can also be seen as the justified costs of achieving a worthwhile goal, maintaining U.S. superiority and bringing to power a pro-American regime in Iraq.

The same kind of "ends justify the means" logic is used by terrorists, including suicide terrorists. Terrorists are trained to see their goal as supreme, as worth whatever sacrifice is necessary, including the killing of others and the ending of their own lives. Whatever it takes, the ends justify the means.

Of course, outsiders will object that: "Terrorists are willing to kill themselves, their parents are willing to send them out to almost certain death. This is very different from the behavior of young people and their parents in Western societies." At this point we need to step back and rethink past conflicts in the West, such as trench warfare in the First World War, when thousands of young men died in fighting every day. The parents of these fighting men sent them to the front with trepidation and enthusiasm, fear and pride—just as the parents of many terrorists experience a mixture of feelings when their children become committed to the moral order of terrorism.

But, I can hear you raise the objection that: "Trench warfare in the First World War involved people from different countries fighting, whereas terrorists in many cases fight and kill their own nationals. For example, in post-Saddam Iraq suicide terrorists have been targeting other Iraqis. Surely this killing of your own kind is different from the Western, or at least the United States, experience?" But such an objection is blatantly wrong, as clearly shown by terrorist attacks, such as the Oklahoma City bombing, where Americans target Americans, as well as the experience of the American Civil War (1861–1865), during which the armies of the North and the South did enormous damage to one another, pitting American against American, sometimes family members against one another.

THE PROCESS OF MORAL ENGAGEMENT

How do individuals become engaged in the morality of terrorism? Through what process does a seventeen-year-old boy, with a love of soccer and life, become convinced that it is morally right that he should strap on an explosive belt and blow himself up in a crowded restaurant? Although this process is unique to terrorism, some of its basic elements are known to us through thousands of studies on how individuals can be influenced by the groups they join—how "rebellious" students of today become conservative members of law firms, how the marines make "fighting machines" out of boys and girls, how cults transform independent individuals into highly obedient followers … and on and on. The social world is filled with examples of how becoming a group member changes the identity of the individual to become more like other group members: to conform and to obey.

In most situations, conformity and obedience have highly beneficial outcomes, allowing small groups and large organizations to carry out tasks efficiently. After all, how could any human groups function effectively without a minimum level of conformity and obedience? Of course, nonconformity and disobedience also serve important constructive functions; "thinking outside the box" and "marching to the beat of a different drum" is sometimes associated with higher levels of creativity and new discoveries. A challenge, then, for all societies is to achieve a balance; to allow a sufficient level of nonconformity and disobedience so that healthy change can take place, without allowing nonconformity and disobedience to become destructive.

A healthy balance will enable individuals to achieve affiliation and belonging, but at the same time leave them room to move in new directions. Unfortunately, the societies of the Near and Middle East are very far from achieving such a balance. A consequence is that young people seek out alternative paths to experience affiliation and belonging.

The process of moral engagement for the potential terrorist begins where many other group processes begin, with the need for affiliation.[32] In most instances individuals become involved in the morality of terrorist groups by becoming involved with others who already are engaged with this morality. In this sense, becoming a terrorist is similar to becoming a member of a religious cult, or an urban street gang, or even a competitive sports team. An individual is attracted by the sense of belonging that the group provides: a need to develop a different, more satisfying identity.

Affiliation

The vast majority of terrorists are young single men (although more women are now being recruited), many of them in their teens. These young men are growing up in societies where most of them have little power, few resources, very little possibility of educational or cultural advancement, no discernable future in terms of solid careers, and no access to female companionship. From the perspective of many of them, all the roads forward seem blocked.

To get a better idea of how different their lives are to what most young men experience in the West, consider the expected developmental path for males aged between fifteen and twenty-five in the United States and other Western societies. What do we expect this age group to be preoccupied with? Whatever list of activities we come up with, dating has to be close to the top of the list. Young men typically become sexually active in the years between fifteen and twenty-five. They find partners and date, although in most cases the relationships they enter will not be long-term. This is the age of infatuations and romances, with relationships sometimes lasting years but typically lasting no more than a few months, or even weeks, and days. But in the societies of the Near and Middle East, young men do not have the freedom to experience romance, because they are kept separated from potential partners. Power and access to sexual partners is in the hands of older men. When we hear of men in Islamic societies having multiple wives, these are typically cases of older men who have accumulated sufficient resources to be able to afford multiple wives.

Traditional societies have their own ways of coping with young men, making sure that they do not cause problems over the many years they need to accumulate resources in order to marry and settle down. By looking at extreme cases, we can get a better idea of the challenge.

Consider the case of the traditional Tiwi society of Northern Australia, for example, where men typically did not have the resources to marry a young wife until they are well past thirty years old.[33] In traditional Tiwi society, the young women married much older men, while younger men either did not have wives, or if they did get married their wives were much older than themselves. So how did traditional Tiwi society control the young men? What did they do to keep the lid on the hot passions of the young? The traditional Tiwi solution was to literally kidnap young men and keep them separate from the rest of society for about a decade during their maturing years, to train them to rejoin society as conformist adults, ready to accept the status quo and the higher power of the older males.

The kidnapping of the young Tiwi male would take place with the complicity or at least tacit acceptance of the boy's father, who may not want his own son kidnapped, but is satisfied knowing that all the other boys (potential competitors for partners) are also being kidnapped and kept out of circulation. A typical kidnapping is described as follows:

Though the father instigated and stage managed the whole affair, he and his household were always thunderstruck when the cross-cousins—armed to the teeth and painted like a war party—arrived at his camp one evening and proceeded to carry off forcibly the yelling 14-year old. He had to be dragged literally from the bosom of his family, with his mother screaming and trying to hide him and the father pretending to resist the invaders to his household. From then on, until the final stage (Mikingula) at age 24–26, the boy was completely under the authority of the men who carried him off. During these approximately 10–12 years, he spent much of the time alone with them in the bush where the group lived a monastic existence, as a small band of isolates, speaking to no one (especially not to females) and obtaining their own food. During these phases the tutors guarded the boy as if he were literally a prisoner and taught him all the things—chiefly ritual matters—that grown men should know. (Hart, et al., 2001, p. 103)

The Tiwi remedy for how to control young bachelors appears extremely harsh to us, but it was an effective way of managing young men and keeping them away from women, in a society controlled by older men who wanted to ensure only they would have access to young women. The young Tiwi men had to be content with life as a member of a "band of brothers," outcasts from the rest of society and particularly from female companionship.

The societies of the Near and Middle East have similar taboos against young men mingling with females other than their close relatives. Imprisonment, fines, public floggings, and even stoning is what awaits people caught having sexual relations out of wedlock. This means that there is huge pressure for men and women to not have romantic relations before marriage.

This was less of a problem in past eras, when people married at a younger age. But a combination of rising expectations, exploding populations, and scarce resources has meant that people have to wait until they are older to get married. Thus, there are millions more unmarried young men waiting out their time, moving in and out of male friendship networks, meeting the basic need for affiliation.

Comradeship, brotherhood, belonging, and a sense of identity through friendship ... these are the basic building blocks, the first steps of young men becoming ensnared in the morality of terrorist organizations. Most terrorists first become engaged in the morality of terrorism through their affiliation with other young people who are connected with terrorist networks. This affiliation comes about through gatherings on street corners, at places of worship, teahouses, and in general where young men are permitted to "hang out."

Secrecy

After an individual has developed friendships with people who actually or potentially are sympathetic toward terrorist networks, three parallel processes evolve. First, through affiliation and comradeship, the young man spends time with his new friends and develops extraordinarily strong bonds with other group members. It is very difficult to understand the importance of male companionship and group life for young men in these societies, when we look at the situation from a Western viewpoint—which is the only viewpoint we have. In the Western context, the best analogy is to consider boys around six to nine years of age, when the boys are strictly segregated from the girls. Of course, in the Western context preteen boys and girls segregate out of choice, whereas in the Near and Middle East men and women in their teens and twenties are forced to segregate; they have no choice. But what is similar in the two cases is the intensity and focus of the male-only experience (and the corresponding female-only experience).

Second, as time passes the young man and the group share ideas and opinions about their problems, hopes, aspirations, and their society and the larger world. In the Near and Middle East context, these discussions inevitably lead to the frustrations of the hundreds of millions of people on the ground floor, and the idea that there seems no way to improve the situation through legitimate means. Their national governments are corrupt and in the pockets of foreign powers, particularly the Americans.

Again, the experiences of young men in Western societies does not provide a good guide for understanding life in male friendship networks in the Near and Middle East. A first fundamental difference is that in the Near and Middle East context, young men are far closer to the practical problems of everyday life—the lack of resources, the lack of educational and job opportunities, and politics at both national and international levels. The teenage boys throwing stones and running through the streets of Near and Middle East cities are more politically aware than most adults in Western societies, not because they read more or are more knowledgeable about abstract political ideas, but because they have felt the crack of the policeman's stick on their heads.

But the Near and Middle East is a place where political views and political ideas have to be well guarded, because they can quickly land a person in jail, or worse. One learns from a young age to trust very few people when it comes to politics: never tell outsiders what you really think, that is the number one rule of survival. The repression of the authorities has a powerful effect on the groups of young men: they develop into secret networks. Even when they are not primarily or even marginally political, they remain insular and secretive.

Thus, the separation of young men and their lives in male-only groups, secretive and segregated, serves as the cultural platform on which terrorist groups build in the Near and Middle East.

Isolation

The turn toward engagement with the morality of terrorism comes about in part through isolation of the male-only group. Isolation and secrecy are natural consequences of severe repression by local authorities. Through a gradual process, the idea that "the ends justify the means" enters and gains influence in the group and the legitimacy of "attacks on selected targets" becomes accepted.

Isolation of the group has a number of consequences.

Because group members do not get to directly test their views of reality against the views of outsiders, and do not open themselves up to external criticism, their worldview never experiences a reality check. Guided by a group leader, typically strong and charismatic, the group members go down a path that eventually leads them to a distinct and often idiosyncratic and incorrect view of reality. For example, the insularity and isolation of the group does not allow for the testing of ideas such as: "Most people in our society are asleep, politically naive, and need a shock to wake them up" and "If people recognize how weak and vulnerable the government is, then they will find the courage to revolt and overthrow the regime."

Cut off from the rest of society, the group evolves a distinct set of norms and rules that strictly regulates the behavior of group members. Almost a century of psychological research demonstrates that, irrespective of the extent to which they are correct, norms function as a powerful force ingroup behavior.[34] Individuals will change their own beliefs and values to conform to the group norm, even in cases when they can clearly recognize that the group norm is incorrect. For example, even when individual members independently think that exploding a bomb in a crowded bus is morally wrong, in the group setting they are far more likely to follow the lead of an authority figure and endorse such a terrorist act.

Under some conditions, individual group members change their behavior to conform to riskier behaviors. In these situations, a great deal is determined by leadership, both the local leader inside the group and the leadership the group accepts from the outside. Unfortunately, the kinds of individuals who come into leadership positions in such situations typically endorse extremist actions. This is in part because the official, government endorsed leaders have been tainted by their associations with the United States and other foreign powers. In countries such as Saudi Arabia, they are seen as U.S. stooges, and their presence creates opportunities for radicals to grab attention by taking up anti-U.S. positions. A consequence for group behavior is that radicals can influence isolated male-only groups to take riskier and riskier positions.

Research on "groupthink" shows that the intelligence of individual group members will not save the isolated, secretive group from adopting disastrously wrong strategies. Again and again, both historical experience and research shows that groups that make decisions in isolation and secrecy tend to become divorced from reality, and to become vulnerable to catastrophic mistakes. To the list of historic examples, such as President Lyndon Johnson and his advisors during the Vietnam years, we can now add President George W. Bush and his advisors and their management of the war in Iraq. In each case, a group of intelligent individuals came up with disastrous plans, in large part because the group worked in ultrasecret conditions and did not open up to feedback from the outside. In terms of sociopsychological processes, groups that veer toward terrorism are similar: they develop wildly incorrect views of the world and implement disastrous plans of action.

Fear

The isolated and secretive all-male group that gradually comes to adopt a morality condoning terrorism is characterized by fear related to two sources, internal and external to the group. On the one hand, group members learn to fear rejection, reprisals, and punishment from others inside their group. On the other hand, there is fear of discovery and harsh treatment at the hands of authorities external to the group.

The need for affiliation provides the initial impetus for individuals to join groups that evolve a morality condoning terrorism. Fear of rejection from the group is an important factor leading individuals to conform and obey. Gradually, as the individuals become absorbed into the secretive life and value system of the group, and as the group takes on riskier and riskier positions, it becomes more and more difficult for individuals to back out. The exit door begins to close. Individual group members fear what would happen to them if they did try to back out, and others fear about their own safety if "deserters" talk to the authorities.

The total dedication of the individual to the group, often achieved through self-denigration and "self-denial" exercises, leaves group members extremely exposed. Each individual announces allegiance to the group cause, and arrives at a situation where his safety and life depends completely on the other group members. The vulnerability of the individual group members means that they are exposed and open to criticism.

The "pressure cooker" atmosphere inside the all-male group is exaggerated by fear of repressions and reprisals on the part of government authorities. The group leader does not need to work hard to keep his group members focused on this external threat; the harsh, dictatorial governments of the Near and Middle East do the job for him. The closed, police-states of the region provide no meaningful opportunities for ordinary people to voice their opinions on social, economic, political, and moral issues, or to participate in any meaningful way in decision making on such matters that impact on their everyday lives. Anyone who steps out of line must fear for his life, because the authorities have proven again and again that they are ruthless. Consequently, group members have a valid reason to fear the threat from government authorities.

EXITING THE THIRD FLOOR

Individuals arrive on the third floor with a strong sense of inadequate identity and dissatisfaction with the way things are. They feel that the world is an unjust place, that the main reasons for prevailing injustices are the United States, Israel, and other external forces, and that local governments in Islamic societies are corrupt and in the pockets of "Satans," great and small. Moreover, by the time individuals arrive on the third floor, they feel convinced that there are no doors open to them, no places or avenues through which their voices could be heard, no ways for them to participate in decision making. On the contrary, any attempt by them to exercise choice in the political arena will be met with fierce repression.

On the third floor, individual males are directed by the norms and rules of their societies to become isolated in male-only groups. From the early teens to the time they get married, males are separated from the opposite sex and segregated in male-only bands to develop rigid, gender-based identities. Given the lack of educational, social, and career opportunities for many young men, their groups inevitably, but often secretly, veer into politics. The isolation and segregation they experience creates conditions for high conformity and obedience within groups, and increases the possibility that riskier and riskier moral values and behavior will be adopted.

The greatest change on the third floor is the increased probability that male-only groups, high on conformity, obedience, and risk-taking, and isolated from the moderating influence of mainstream society, will adopt a morality supportive of terrorism. This morality sees the ends justifying the means, categorizes the world into "us" versus "them," and condones all means by which "the enemy" could be destroyed or weakened toward defeat. As the group moves further along the endorsement of a terrorist morality, secrecy and isolation increase, and the risks and fears of discovery become exaggerated in the minds of group members. Under these conditions, the power of the group leader further increases, making it more possible that moral thinking condoning terrorism will translate into terrorist acts.

CHAPTER 8

Fourth Floor: It's Us against Them

From among the individuals who incorporate the morality of terrorism in their identities on the third floor, some climb up to the fourth floor and enter the secret world of terrorist organizations. These individuals have evolved identities that find fulfillment and meaning through a morality that depicts only one goal as worth living for, and justifies killing civilians to get to that one goal. For the "Black Tigers" who specialize in suicide terrorism in Sri Lanka, that one goal is independence and justice for a Tamil homeland. For Hamas, that goal is the establishment of a Palestinian homeland. For Al Qaeda, this one goal is the ideal Islamic society, as interpreted by bin Laden and various groups of fundamentalists, including *Salafists* ("purists").

The morality that guides terrorists justifies using every means available in order to reach the desired goal. Captured Islamic terrorists report believing that when they die and reach the next world, they will be forgiven for killing civilians because "it was justified." From the terrorists' point of view, their ends justify their means, both in this world and the next.

It is often said by leaders in the West that the "war on terror" is about winning hearts and minds, rather than just bullets and tanks. Insofar as this approach leads to a focus on a moral struggle central to identity, it is correct. However, moralities and identities do not arise out of a vacuum, they arise out of particular social, political, and economic conditions and they spread because of those conditions; it is to these conditions that we must attend.

The Land of No Return

After a recruit has stepped into the network of terrorist organizations, there is little or no opportunity for him or her to leave alive. Psychologically, the recruit completes the adoption of a terrorist identity and the process of immersion into a world of rigid categorical thinking, "its us versus them," "kill or be killed." The behavior of recruits closely parallels this thinking, so that information is closely guarded within very small, tightly knit groups. Even close family and friends are kept in the dark about the secret world into which the recruit has entered. Consequently, after a terrorist bomber has struck, the typical reaction from wives, mothers, and close friends is often complete bewilderment. After the July 7, 2005, terrorist attacks in London, the family of the four attackers universally declared their disbelief that such young men, soccer and cricket lovers and devoted husbands and fathers among them, would commit such crimes. How could they? They must have been duped. Surely if it was otherwise, family and friends around them would have recognized what was going on?

But this line of thinking fails to consider the complete compartmentalization that takes place in the minds of recruits to terrorist organizations. They rigidly separate the terrorist, criminal compartment of their thinking and activities from the ordinary, everyday compartment. These are two worlds that never meet in the actions and thoughts of recruits. Thus, the twenty-two-year old soccer and cricket lover and the nineteen-year-old caring father and husband go about their everyday lives without giving the slightest hint of their parallel existence as recruits to terrorist organizations.

Having entered a secret and dangerous land, recruits find there is no possibility of return. The difficulty of return is in large part related to the issue of safety and security: other members of the terrorist organization would see it as dangerous if a recruit took the exit strategy and "gave up" their membership. A "deserter" could bring down an entire terrorist network. Immersion in secret small-group activities leads to changes in and solidification of certain points of view among recruits:

- a legitimization of the terrorist organization and its goals;
- a belief that the ends justify the means;
- reinforcement of categorical "us versus them" view of the world;
- exaggerated belief that they are about to undertake "great" feats.

Along with these changes in outlook and beliefs, the recruit also finds a specialized role in the terrorist network. The particular role a recruit takes up depends in large part on individual motivation, talents, timing, and the special needs of the terrorist group. Some individuals have leadership aspirations and skills, and a few of these individuals eventually become terrorist cell managers and work to "inspire" and guide others. At the other extreme are recruits who only serve as "fodder," to be used as suicide bombers, with or without their explicit knowledge.

Very little attention has been given to the many different specialized roles that have evolved in terrorist networks. From the popular media, the impression one gets is that there are basically two types of terrorists: first, there are the "evil masterminds" and, second, there are the thousands of suicide terrorists who carry out the attacks, planned and ordered by the evil masterminds. But terrorist networks and terrorist organizations can only function at local, national, and international levels through specialization of roles and an appropriate level of training and information for individuals who serve in the different specialty positions. Consequently, we must pay closer attention to the evolving specialized roles of terrorists.

It is after a person has reached the fourth floor and been recruited as a terrorist that training for a specialized role begins in earnest. In some cases, the training involves limited skills and very little information, and the main investment is in convincing the recruit of the moral purpose and correctness of the terrorist operation about to be attempted. An example of this minimal investment is sometimes the recruit trained to serve as the "mule" or "carrier" of explosives, who is sacrificed in order to blow up a bus, or a train, or some other target. At the other extreme, the work involves months and sometimes years of training a recruit to achieve a higher level of expertise in a specialized area. An example is when a recruit, who typically has some level of special knowledge and aptitude, is given specialized training in areas such as electronics and explosives.

In discussing the following specialized roles, I do not mean to imply that recruits are placed in particular roles and they rigidly remain in those roles. Obviously, there is some movement of recruits from one role to another within and across terrorist organizations and networks. Movement across roles and *role enlargement*, expanding the responsibilities of a particular role and taking on additional roles, does take place, particularly among those recruits who have longer involvements in terrorist networks. Such movement obviously does not take place in the case of recruits who "successfully" serve in the role of suicide bombers.

SPECIALIZED ROLES IN TERRORIST CELLS AND NETWORKS

Over the last few decades, researchers have correctly come to the conclusion that there is no simple causal explanation for terrorism. For example, it has been pointed out that poverty and low education do not cause terrorism, that the motive for terrorism can be religious or secular, national or international, and that the role of "causal factors" tend to be complex and indirect. The same line of thinking has led many researchers to conclude that it is not useful to try to defeat terrorism by focusing on individual terrorists and their intrapersonal character- istics, because as long as the context remains the same, each individ- ual terrorist who is removed will immediately be replaced by another individual.

The focus on context is correct, but it should not lead us to completely dismiss the specialized roles that have evolved in terrorist organizations and networks. It is these specialized roles that allow terrorist operations to be implemented effectively, and sometimes with a lot of precision. In identifying and assessing types of terrorists on the basis of in-depth and critical readings of the literature on terrorism, I have found it useful to apply the following criteria:

1. *Asset*: what is the main asset that the individual brings to the organization?
2. *Function*: what function(s) does the individual serve in the orga- nization?
3. *Service length*: what is the time frame for the service that the individual provides the organization?
4. *Means of contact*: how does the individual contact others in the organization?
5. *Contact with public*: does the terrorist have overt contact with the public, or remain covert?
6. *Expertise*: what level of expertise does the terrorist have?
7. *Demographic characteristics*: what are the typical demographic characteristics of the terrorist?
8. *Location*: where is the terrorist located?
9. *Motivation*: what is the main motivation of the terrorist?
10. *Psychological marker*: what is the most salient psychological marker of the terrorist?

My research led to the identification of the following major special- ized roles among terrorists: (A) source of inspiration (B) strategist (C) networker (D) expert (E) cell manager (F) local agitator and guide (G) local cell member (H) fodder, and (I) fund-raiser.

Before discussing the characteristics of each specialized role, it is im- portant to point out that in many instances one individual will fill more than one specialized role. For example, a cell manager could also serve as an expert (in explosives, for example), as well as a networker. However, in some organizations and in some situations, each specialized role is filled by a single person.

Specialized Terrorist Roles

A. *Terrorist Type:* Source of inspiration

Example: Osama bin Laden[35]

Summary Description: Most terrorists are inspired by a leader or set of leaders, who serve as a guide and a *source of inspiration* for both the terrorist group and individual members. For example, particularly since the tragedy of September 11, Osama bin Laden has served as a source of inspiration for thousands of terrorists and would-be terrorists in many different countries. Thanks to modern electronic communications, his image and speeches have been flashed around the world. There are also such sources of inspiration for domestic terrorists in the United States. For example Matt Hale, former leader of the white supremacist World Church of the Creator, served as an inspiration for a lethal terrorist attack on a federal judge.

An important characteristic of a source of inspiration is that specific orders and directives for specific attacks do not have to be issued to followers. Rather, the source stands for a broad value system and worldview. Messages from the source tend to be expansive and often attempt to present the source as a "statesman." But the declared values and pronouncements of the source create an atmosphere in which those who are inspired know what they are expected to do: that is, attack and destroy their opponents. Just by being there, the source influences thoughts and actions in a particular direction.

Sources of inspiration for terrorists tend to be "oppositional leaders," meaning that they stand against certain things and position themselves as being against large movements and forces, such as "American imperialism."

1. *Asset:* The greatest asset that a source of inspiration brings to a terrorist movement is well known to the advertising industry: name recognition. Paradoxically, this recognition is bestowed to the source of inspiration by the Western dominated modern mass media—at the same time that the source of inspiration condemns modern mass media as Satanic, he is willing to use it for his own purposes. Osama bin Laden has become a household name through the modern mass media, and Al Qaeda uses the World Wide Web to transmit messages both to its followers and to the larger world.

2. *Function:* The main function of the source of inspiration is to serve as a symbolic figurehead. After the passage of time and the

accumulation of speeches, writings, and edicts from the source of inspiration, it does not much matter if he is alive or dead. His worldview serves as a guide. Similarly, there does not need to be an organization such as Al Qaeda with a physical presence. Al Qaeda and Osama bin Laden serve as sources of inspiration and guides, irrespective of whether they continue to exist in actuality; they have become guiding ideas. To defeat these ideas, we must change the conditions that lead to support for these ideas.

3. *Service length:* Sources of inspiration tend to serve the purposes of terrorist organizations for very long time periods, often because they continue to serve a purpose even after they are dead and buried. This is particularly true in cases where the source of inspiration has guided followers through his writings.

4. *Means of contact:* A variety of means are used by the source of inspiration to contact others. On the one hand, a wide range of mass media, including electronic communications, is used to reach as large an audience as possible. For example, Osama bin Laden and other such leaders have used the Web in this way. On the other hand, secretive messengers are used to hand deliver messages to and from the source of inspiration.

5. *Contact with public:* The source of inspiration plays as public a role as possible, to reach as many people as possible, even though he may be in hiding from authorities.

6. *Expertise:* The persons who fill this role are generalists rather than specialists. They tend to have gained extensive worldly experience.

7. *Demographic characteristics:* Sources of inspiration are males who are middle-aged or older.

8. *Location:* In most cases locations are unknown.

9. *Motivation:* Sources of inspiration respond to social demands for messianic leaders, motivated to achieve change on a grand, historic scale.

10. *Psychological marker:* Paradoxical sense of self is the most important psychological marker of the source of inspiration. On the one hand, he speaks as an all-powerful leader who can unleash terrifying forces on the world. On the other hand, he is a victim and one of the downtrodden: David facing Goliath.

B. *Terrorist Type:* Strategist

Example: Ayman Zawahiri (bin Laden's Deputy)[36]

Summary Description: Strategists do not have the charisma and public appeal of the source of inspiration, and they tend to do their work quietly and in the background rather than in the limelight. However, their role is essential in helping the source of inspiration to be more effective.

1. *Asset:* The strategist's most important asset is as thinker and planner.
2. *Function:* The function of the strategist is to make planning and management more effective.
3. *Service length:* Strategists tend to be long-term survivors and providers of services to other terrorists.
4. *Contact type:* Strategists remain in the shadows and maintain covert and limited contact with a small number of other terrorists.
5. *Contact with public:* Strategists tend to try to limit their contact with the public.
6. *Expertise:* Strategists tend to have higher levels of expertise and specialization in areas such as finance.
7. *Demographic characteristics:* Strategists tend to be middle-aged, and to be looked up to as "smart."
8. *Location:* Strategists can live almost anywhere in the world, including in Western societies.
9. *Motivation:* Strategists enjoy being the "power behind the throne," quietly wielding influence.
10. *Psychological marker:* The most distinct psychological marker of the strategist is detachment and the ability to provide plans and give advice sometimes leading to multiple deaths, without themselves becoming emotionally involved in the process or outcome.

C. *Terrorist Type:* Networker

Example: Abu al-Janna (a Syrian who has acted as a networker for terrorists operating in the Near East).[37]

Summary Description: Networkers are able to blend in with different populations and move from place to place without attracting attention. They may use a "front," such as a business, and travel through normal transportation routes, or they may use routes not known to the general public. There are an almost infinite variety of strategies they use to help create and maintain networks of contacts between terrorists and their supporters, rather similar to strategies used by drug traffickers.

1. *Asset:* The networker's most valuable asset is mobility, made possible by anonymity. Second, networkers are good "readers" of both

people and social situations. Third, some networkers use computer skills to develop and expand contacts.

2. *Function:* Networkers are the glue that holds terrorist cells and individuals together, enabling the expression of terrorism as a movement rather than a series of isolated incident. Without networkers, Al Qaeda would remain an idea.

3. *Service length:* The demands of the job require that networkers gain sufficient experience and local knowledge of different recruitment centers. Their service length tends to be over ten years.

4. *Contact type:* Networkers maintain a regular pattern of contacts; they continually test out new contacts and resources.

5. *Contact with public:* Networkers are able to move through public places and situations without attracting attention to themselves. When they have contact with the public, they are not recognized in their terrorist roles.

6. *Expertise*: Networkers are the communications experts of terrorism; some of them have computer skills, but they also rely on old-fashioned methods of traveling from one location to another in order to deliver messages.

7. *Demographic characteristics*: Networkers tend to be males aged from the late twenties to the forties. They are physically fit, but old enough to have experience of different demanding situations.

8. *Location*: Networkers vary a great deal in terms of the geographical range they work in. Some of them network within relatively small areas, such as a neighborhood or a small town. Others travel across countries and continents and are international networkers.

9. *Motivation*: The main motivation of networkers is social—the excitement of travel, and keeping up a double life while interacting with different people in different places.

10. *Psychological marker*: The most salient psychological marker for networkers is the ability to live two parallel lives over many years, sometimes over decades. At the same time that they are extroverted and gregarious, they maintain a private, secret side to their lives.

D. Terrorist Type: Expert

Example: Mustafa Setmarian Nasar (also known as Abu Musab Suri), who has used the Web to spread information about weapons and tactics.[38]

Summary Description: Terrorist groups are making increasing use of modern electronic equipment, more sophisticated weapons systems, and coordinated tactical attacks requiring demanding planning. There has been some tendency to make use of specialized skills and aptitudes, and to focus on increasingly specialized training and task allocation. The result is the emergence of a cadre of "experts," who take on the title of "engineer."

1. *Asset:* The most important asset that experts bring to terrorist movements is their ability to complete a narrow task, such as setting the appropriate size and timing for explosives, effectively in a speedy and covert manner.
2. *Function:* Experts function to maximize the effectiveness of terrorist groups, by using specialized skills to help the group carry out specific operations.
3. *Service length:* Experts tend to have had a shorter career span in terrorism than do networkers, sometimes being put to work as experts very soon after recruitment.
4. *Contact type:* Because they have valued skills that are needed in different places, experts tend to work with more than one cell. For example, experts in explosives work with different groups to prepare suicide bombers. Often, networkers prepare the ground for experts to work with different cells.
5. *Contact with public:* There is no overt contact between experts and the public; they remain in camouflage, and in this way also they are similar to networkers.
6. *Expertise:* The most specialized and focused among types of terrorists are the experts.
7. *Demographic characteristics:* Experts tend to be males in their late twenties and thirties. They have grown up in the computer age and often have higher level technical education and experience.
8. *Location:* Individuals who fill the role of experts are often very close to the action, but because of their valued skills, serious efforts are made to keep them out of danger. In most cases, experts help set up and launch an operation, but always try to keep their distance from the heat of the conflict.
9. *Motivation:* Professionalism and satisfaction in getting a technical job done, rather like the feeling of satisfaction that skilled programmers or mechanics have when they tackle a tough technical job.
10. *Psychological marker:* The key psychological marker of the expert is emotional detachment and satisfaction with technical prowess. The suicide bomber, like many terrorists on the front line, only

face a killing situation once. The expert sets up killings again and again, and so needs a higher level of detachment to continue to operate.

E. Terrorist Type: Cell manager

Example: Mohammed Atta, the person believed to have assembled and managed the nineteen hijackers responsible for terrorist attacks on September 11, 2001.[39]

Summary Description: The cell manager is the workhorse of terrorist organizations. This is the "jack of all trades" of the local cell, who also serves as a recruiter, trainer, link with outsiders, and an inspired leader. The role of the cell manager evolved with the emergence of the cell as the basic building block of terrorist movements. This development probably has its roots in post-World War Two revolutionary movements that used terrorist tactics to fight dictatorships in Latin America.

1. *Asset:* The cell manager's greatest asset is his all-round leadership ability, as a father figure, a friend, and also as a disciplinarian who maintains order and discipline in the group. The successful cell manager is able to foresee and prevent future defections on the part of dissatisfied group members.
2. *Function:* Cell managers function to ensure the continuation, security, and effective functioning of the terrorist cell. This is a very demanding task, particularly because numerous national and international antiterrorism agencies with enormous resources continually attempt to infiltrate and destroy terrorist cells.
3. *Service length:* The cell manager can serve in this role anything from a few years to a few decades.
4. *Contact type:* Cell managers have to be open to the possibility of attracting new recruits, but at the same time they must guard against infiltration by antiterrorist agents. Thus, although cell managers work in strict secrecy, they are particularly vulnerable when new group members are being recruited, when existing members might be motivated to defect, and when the cell manager is engaged in the task of contacting the managers of other cells.
5. *Contact with public:* The operations of the cell manager are covert and he does not have overt contact with the public.
6. *Expertise:* The demands of the job mold the cell manager into an all-rounder, even though he might have special knowledge in a particular domain.
7. *Demographic characteristics:* Cell managers tend to vary in age from the late twenties to the mid-forties.

8. *Location:* In urban centers, typically close to access to the best transportation networks.

9. *Motivation:* Cell managers enjoy a leadership role, social relationships, male bonding, and discipline. In a military context, the cell manager might be a tough but respected Sergeant.

10. *Psychological marker:* The cell manager is the person who, if the cell is destroyed, will have the psychological inclination and skills to begin anew and build up the cell again.

F. Terrorist Type: Local agitator and guide

Example: Abubakar Baasyir, Muslim preacher operating in Jakarta, Indonesia.[40]

Summary Description: Although a "source of inspiration," such as Osama bin Laden, can serve to attract new recruits to terrorist movements, such an "international figure" could not guide potential recruits at the local level. The "local agitator and guide" both leads dissatisfied individuals, typically young men, to move toward a morality condoning terrorism, and also points such individuals in directions that put them in touch with terrorist recruiters. In the context of Islamic societies, in many cases the local agitators and guides serve as preachers or teachers.

1. *Asset:* Local agitators and guides have detailed information and contacts in the local community, and they are particularly good in interpersonal communications.

2. *Function:* Local agitators and guides serve to move dissatisfied individuals in the direction of terrorism, toward potential recruiters linked directly or indirectly to terrorist cells and/or operations.

3. *Service length:* Although these individuals are locally recognized as "hot heads," they do not burn up and fizzle out early, but tend to have long careers, often with decades of activity in the same community.

4. *Contact type:* Local agitators and guides tend to work more in the open, but also tend to have covert relations with a few contacts operating in or close to terrorist operations and cells.

5. *Contact with public:* Local agitators and guides have very open and covert relations with the public.

6. *Expertise:* Local agitators and guides are expert communicators within the local community, and have invaluable information about local sentiments and trends.

7. *Demographic characteristics:* These individuals tend to be in the late thirties to the late fifties.

8. *Location:* Local agitators and guides are at the center of local community activities and have a very public, although not always welcome, role in local affairs.
9. *Motivation:* The main motivation for local agitators and guides is to instigate change, but often in a reactionary manner, away from globalization trends.
10. *Psychological marker:* These are extroverted, charismatic individuals, routinely and publicly expressing dissatisfaction with trends in culture and values.

G. Terrorist Type: Local cell member

Example: Sher Ali, a Pakistani cell member captured in Afghanistan.[41]

Summary Description: The foot soldiers who carry out all of the often tedious work involved in terrorist attacks make up the local cell members. The work involved can be laborious, because surveillance and detailed information gathering is often undertaken before terrorist attacks. In most cases, individuals become cell members after having acquired at least some key elements of the proterrorism morality. However, it is within the cell that socialization and learning to become an active terrorist takes place. Cell members acquire the subculture of the cell (for example, norms about nicknames, group member roles, and special safety codes), including the disciplinary rules (forms of punishment, such as being given particularly menial tasks, being ostracized for a period of time), as well as procedures for maintaining secrecy.

1. *Asset:* The local cell member is loyal and obedient, but at the same time does not have expertise at a high level and therefore is relatively easily replaceable.
2. *Function:* To work in a group to carry out terrorist operations and provide support for experts and leaders.
3. *Service length:* From a few months to a few years.
4. *Contact type:* The local cell member often lives a parallel life, working and living in a community at the same time as maintaining support for the cell.
5. *Contact with public:* As little contact as possible with the public, and almost always under the umbrella of the cell and its leader.
6. *Expertise:* Some role specialization within the cell (for example, specializing in being the "lookout" before and during attacks), but does not have a high level of expertise.
7. *Demographic characteristics:* Typically from the early twenties to the thirties.

8. *Location:* In major urban centers, close to where attacks take place, or at least has access to transportation system.
9. *Motivation:* Often motivated to join the cell through friendship and family affiliations.
10. *Psychological marker:* Average or below average intelligence, loyal, and dedicated to the group leader.

H. Terrorist Type: Fodder

Example: Sajida Mubarak al-Rishawi, the thirty-five-year-old Iraqi woman who tried unsuccessfully to blow herself up in a hotel in Amman, Jordan, in November 2005.[42]

Summary Description: The suicide bomber is the most well publicized type of terrorist I refer to as "fodder," a title chosen because these individuals are seen by the leadership of the terrorist organization as expendable. Often, they are recruited for a specific terrorist attack and are given information only about small aspects of that one operation, which might take no more than twenty-four hours. Within those twenty-four hours, the recruited individual receives a great deal of positive attention and is treated as a kind of celebrity, particularly by the recruiter (who stays by his side constantly) and by a charismatic cell leader. Fodder will also be recruited and used to distract attention from a more important terrorist attacker. For example, when an explosives expert is setting equipment into position, a fodder may be positioned ready to attack security forces if they arrive on the scene and might capture the expert. In such cases, the fodder may be killed or captured.

1. *Asset:* Is expendable and willing to obey orders.
2. *Function:* Attack and inflict maximum damage.
3. *Service length:* Often very brief; sometimes no more than a few days.
4. *Contact type:* As brief a contact as possible with other active terrorists.
5. *Contact with public:* Brief and covert.
6. *Expertise:* None.
7. *Demographic characteristics:* Typically males in their teens and early twenties, increasing use of females in order to slip through security screens.
8. *Location:* Recruited very close to where the attack will take place.
9. *Motivation:* To be accepted as a group member, as a comrade, to receive attention, and to become a hero, even momentarily, in the eyes of significant others.

10. *Psychological marker:* Typically low in intelligence: a complex mixture of fervor and frustration, hope and hopelessness.

I. Terrorist Type: Fund-raiser

Example: Mohamad Noordin Top, a fund-raiser and recruiter for terrorist networks active in Indonesia.[43]

Summary description: On the one hand, terrorism does not require much funding and even major terrorist attacks, including September 11, involve thousands rather than millions of dollars changing hands. A major reason for the low cost is that at least some terrorists "work for free" and do not expect to receive payment for their services. Thus, the payroll of terrorist organizations is far, far lower than the payroll of the national and international organizations fighting terrorism. On the other hand, terrorist movements need funding for operations and equipment, as well as "educational" and training programs. Modern terrorism increasingly relies on computer technology, lasers, and electronic equipment to carry out tasks ranging from setting off explosions to making false documents, and all this requires hard cash. Thus, despite a "dedicated work force" willing to forego wages, fund-raising does have an important role in terrorist movements. With the crackdown of antiterrorist agents on fund-raising in both East and West, fund-raisers for terrorist movements have gone underground and raise money through clandestine means, a route particularly suitable to the Near and Middle East societies where a great deal of business is conducted in informal rather than formal ways.

As in the case of Northern Ireland and other regions where terrorists have operated, in the Islamic world fund-raising for terrorist operations is closely associated with traditional criminal activities, such as the drug trade, kidnapping, and extortion. This is particularly the case in Afghanistan and Iraq, as it was historically in the heyday of terrorist groups in Latin America back in the 1950–1970 period.

Despite the wide variety of sources and methods used to gather funds to support terrorist activities, it is still possible to identify a set of individuals who serve as fund-raisers for terrorist movements. These individuals have learned to avoid leaving paper trails, sometimes by transferring money using diamonds, gold, and other valuable commodities.

1. *Asset:* The fund-raiser is at the center of social, religious, and political networks, but is seldom overtly political and has the ability to stay under the radar.

2. *Function:* To gather funds from different sources, to remain "under the radar," and to channel resources to support terrorist movements and operations.

3. *Service length:* Fund-raisers are long-term supporters of the morality of terrorism, but their fund-raising activities are often inconsistent and go through cycles of high or low or no activity, depending on political conditions and financial opportunities.

4. *Contact type:* Fund-raisers go through intermediaries and often do not have direct contact with active terrorists.

5. *Contact with public:* In the post-9/11 climate, fund-raisers are covert operators and try hard to avoid paper trails.

6. *Expertise:* These individuals acquire a medium level of expertise in commercial and financial networking.

7. *Demographic characteristics:* Fund-raisers tend to be mostly males, but sometimes also females, typically middle-aged, and older.

8. *Location:* In Western societies, fund-raisers are located in immigrant neighborhoods, and are often involved in trade and charity activities.

9. *Motivation:* These individuals are ideologically committed to the causes and morality of particular terrorist movements, but are not motivated to achieve personal fame or glory.

10. *Psychological marker:* Outwardly conservative and conformist, but highly ethnocentric and radical in their beliefs, which they express only in very private interactions.

EXITING THE FOURTH FLOOR: THE TERRORISM ICEBERG

By the time individuals are ready to exit from the fourth floor, they have experienced a further change in their identities in response to new social demands in their terrorist cells: they now see themselves as belonging to a terrorist cause, with a specialized role as part of a terrorist group, in a world rigidly divided into "us" and "them," "good" and "evil." Part of the terrorist identity involves camouflage and subversion.

Those exiting the fourth floor have learned how to present the "tip of the iceberg" to the world outside, to keep as much as possible hidden, even from close family and friends. The "iceberg metaphor" is appropriate for terrorist organizations and networks, in the sense that even when terrorist groups are active, outsiders only see the tip of the iceberg protruding out of the water. This "tip of the iceberg" for terrorist organizations and networks is typically (1) the inspirational leader, whose purpose is to become as well known as possible around the world, and (2) the suicide bombers who are killed, or the terrorist "mules" who are not necessarily supposed to get killed but get caught trying to execute an attack. All the other specialists who fill different roles in terrorist organizations and networks, including strategists, networkers, experts, cell managers, local agitators and guides, local cell members, and fund-raisers, try their best to remain hidden "under water." They are the main part of the iceberg that we seldom see, although we know from research and experience that the tip of the iceberg could not stay up if the main body was not present and playing a supporting role under the water.

It is during their stay on the fourth floor that recruits find their places in the network of specialized roles. It is also on this floor that individuals find that their options have narrowed considerably. They are now part of a tightly controlled group that they cannot exit from alive.

CHAPTER 9

Fifth Floor: This "Heroic" Act Will Improve the World

Why war? Why terrorism?

How can we find their root causes and map out solutions?

These questions reflect an assumption that war and terrorism are abnormal, out of the ordinary. We are apt to describe ourselves as a man or woman "of peace" rather than "of war;" we regard peace rather than war as integral to our identities. We assume that peace is healthy, natural, and that war is unhealthy, unnatural.

We do not ask "Why peace?" because we assume that peace is the normal state of affairs, and it is war that is abnormal and in need of understanding. Our assumptions make sense, as long as the behavior we are considering takes place in our kind of "normal" world, and for the most part this is the case.

In my travel and research in different parts of the Western and non-Western world, I have been consistently impressed by how kind, honest, and peace-oriented most people are most of the time. When I moved to Washington D.C., in 1990, the so-called "crime capital of the world," to the amusement of my friends I continued to conform to the stereotype of the "absentminded professor," repeatedly leaving my wallet, keys, and other belongings in public places, several times on sidewalks, for strangers to pick up. Never once did my wallet and other belongings fail to get back to me intact, two times by me receiving a call from a perfect stranger telling me that my wallet had been found and instructing me where to go to pick up my belongings.

Of course there is violent crime in Washington, D.C., just as there is in other major urban centers. But the point I am making is that the general trend in behavior shows people being law abiding, and even going an extra step to help others.

In case you think I am painting too rosy a picture of human behavior, try the following exercise. Stop a stranger in a street in a major city and ask for directions to a location, such as a local shopping mall or a hotel. In the vast majority of cases, strangers will try to help you find the destination you seek.

Surely we must see this as surprising, given that we are living in a competitive world where time and resources matter so much?

Amazing as it may seem, total strangers will give up their time and energy to help us find our way, rather than to mislead us, get us lost, and leave us stranded in this "competitive world." Amazing as it may seem, most people most of the time "do the right thing" toward their fellow humans.

But there is a vitally important requirement for this to happen: there must be a general expectation that this should happen among good people, and most people must see themselves as good. In other words, people will "do the right thing" when it is expected that they should "do the right thing" because they are good. People will help one another and maintain peaceful relations with their fellow humans if the general expectancy is that this is the correct way for good people to behave.

Most people will behave according what is normative for their identities. This comes about because of the power of norms, and the tremendous impact of obedience to authority.

But what about situations in which it becomes normative for good people to harm particular others, to wage war rather than peace, and to destroy rather than to build? In such situations, also, the power of norms is relentless, and obedience to authority is crushing. It is in this light that we should think about the situation on the fifth floor of the staircase to terrorism, and what awaits individuals who climb up to this final floor. When we reach the fifth floor, we must set aside whatever expectations we have about normative thoughts and actions, such as in terms of peaceful and helpful behavior toward strangers.

The key, then, to understanding the behavior of individuals who reach the fifth floor of the staircase to terrorism is to appreciate processes of conformity to norms and obedience to authority. Conformity and obedience exist in all societies, but under certain conditions it becomes integral to identities for people to conform by harming others and to obey orders to kill.

THE POWER OF NORMS

By the time potential terrorists have reached the final floor of the staircase to terrorism, their identities have become immersed in a context that most of us would see as topsy-turvy, with what is defined as "right" in the situation being what most of us see as clearly "wrong." But in order to understand behavior on the fifth floor, we must avoid being mesmerized by the rights and wrongs of behaviors, and focus instead on processes of conformity and obedience that lead to particular types of behaviors. Fortunately, some of the most insightful research in modern psychology is available to guide us to a better understanding on the topic of conformity and obedience.

This research on conformity and obedience suggests that identity is not something static and fixed across contexts. Rather, identity is in important ways highly flexible and shifts with social demands. A person who in situation "A" acts independently, is peace loving, and is concerned not to give offense to others, is transformed in situation "B" into a person who is aggressive, destructive, and willing to kill others. Experimental research suggests ways in which even "ordinary" people can experience such dramatic changes.

Imagine you are a participant in a study, sitting in a dark room with a small group of other people, looking at a spot of light on a black screen. It is as if you are fixating on a single star in the night sky. As you look up, the spot of light, the "star," seems to move. You are not sure how much the light moves, sometimes less and sometimes more, but each time you look its position seems to shift. The researchers running the experiment ask each of you to estimate how much the spot of light moves and record your answers. After repeated showing of the spot of light and repeated estimates, you converge on a "group norm," such as "one inch of movement" or "two inches of movement," and stay close to it for the rest of your estimates.

Next, after a period of few hours or days, you are once again given an opportunity to look at a spot of light in a dark background and to estimate the amount of movement you see, but this time you are in the situation alone. The research question is this: will the "group norm" established in the first situation influence your estimates now that you are on your own?

In order to appreciate the importance of this research question, we need to know that the spot of light never actually moves. Consequently, the "group norm" estimating one inch of movement, two inches of movement, or any other amount of movement, is always wrong.

The results of numerous studies, starting with the pioneering research of the Turkish–American psychologist Muzafer Sherif back in the 1930s, show that even after individual participants are placed in a situation on their own to estimate the movement of dots of light, their estimates are influenced by group-established norms.[44] Like a hidden hand that is unseen yet effective, group-established norms can continue to shape individual actions long after a person has left the group.

The impact of the group on individual estimates is less powerful in situations where individuals first establish personal norms by themselves, and are later placed in a group context. In such cases, it seems that the personal norm can to some degree serve to inoculate the individual against group pressure. However, notice that in the cases of individuals who reach the final floor on the staircase to terrorism, their climb up is step by step, so they become immersed in the morality of terrorism and the norms of terrorist movements through a very gradual process. They seldom have an opportunity to first develop their own norms, and then face the pressure of group-established norms at a later stage.

Moreover, so far we have talked about the role of *spontaneous norms*, norms that evolve naturally in groups without any effort to manipulate norm formation. As individuals move up the staircase to terrorism and reach the fifth floor, they find themselves in groups where they are also influenced by *manipulated norms*, norms explicitly brought about by design. Experimental studies show that group norms can be influenced by planting "radicals" in a group who express extremist views, as in the example of a group member estimating that he saw a spot of light move twelve inches instead of one inch. In such cases, radical estimates can influence group norms even after a radical member has left the group. In the context of the staircase to terrorism, from about the third floor radicals often infiltrate potentially terrorist groups and move group norms toward extremism. In this way, a group of disaffected youth gradually moves toward more extremist positions and accepting the morality of terrorism.

Step-by-Step Terrorist Group Formation

Recruits to terrorist groups are selected with considerable care and are assimilated into groups gradually. Individuals with criminal records and mental disabilities are not recruited, in part because they are seen to increase security risks and also because they would not pass tests of ideological and/or religious purity. The new recruit to a terrorist group finds himself (for it is typically a male) in a situation where the existing members tend to speak with one voice. Thus, even in cases where a new recruit questions the morality condoning terrorism, he is confronted by established group norms.

Research by Solomon Asch in the 1950s, and more recent research using brain imaging technology, demonstrates the enormous power of majority established norms to force an individual to conform.[45] Asch showed groups of participants a standard vertical line, A, which they had to compare to three other vertical lines, B, C, and D, one of which was the same length as A. The participants had to say which of the lines was alike, something they could all do correctly when tested individually.

Each group only included one real "naive" participant; the others were confederates of the researcher. The job of confederates was to unanimously give correct answers when assessing some sets of lines, but incorrect answers when assessing other sets of lines. The confederates always gave their answers prior to the real participant. The research question is this: would participants follow the lead of confederates when confederates gave incorrect answers? The surprising answer is that most participants gave incorrect answers at least once. Cross-cultural research shows that people in the United States are about as conformist as people from other countries, depending on the type of person they are interacting with. For example, compared to Japanese people, Americans tend to be less conformist when interacting with their family, but more conformist when interacting with strangers. Despite some variation across cultures, there is consistency in that a significant number of people conform to incorrect norms. But is this because group pressure actually changed what they saw?

More recent research using brain imaging technology suggests that, indeed, group pressure can alter what people see.[46] This research used the same basic procedures as introduced by Asch: one "naive" participant reported on what he/she saw, after a group of confederates gave a correct or incorrect report of what they saw. Instead of vertical lines, the participants judged similarity of three-dimensional figures. Using functional magnetic resonance imaging (fMRI), a scanner that detects the parts of the brain that are most active when people carry out different tasks, researchers could identify centers of brain activity when the "naive" participants either conformed and gave incorrect answers, or did not conform under group pressure and gave correct answers. The brain scans showed that when participants conformed and gave incorrect answers, the parts of their brains that were most active are centers of vision and spatial perception. The implication is that group pressure led them to actually see the three-dimensional images differently.

Terrorist Organizations as "Total Institutions"

A useful way to better understand the behavior of terrorists is to think of terrorist organizations as total institutions, such as asylums and prisons, where individuals march in time with a collective regiment. The mechanisms of control include norms and authority figures. Erving Goffman's (1922–1982) studies of people in asylums highlights how individuals who are labeled "insane," most often against their will, tend to end up accepting the label they have been assigned and conforming to the norms of the asylum, as a way of winning favor with the authority figures who control their lives and are the gatekeepers to the "free world" outside the asylum.[47] Many of the "patients" try to play the role of "model patient" in order to win release more quickly, even if it means playing the role of a "patient" who is first "mentally ill" and later recovers. Research on behavior in total institutions suggests that individuals will often change their behavior a great deal to fit in, becoming more peaceful, docile, or violent as the situation demands.

This raises questions about people in prisons: to what extent is behavior in prisons an outcome of the particular characteristics of the individual prisoners and guards? For example, is it because prisoners are aggressive and prison guards are sadistic that prisons in the United States (where over two million prisoners "serve time") are in such poor condition? How would ordinary people like you and I cope in a total institution such as a prison? Would we behave "normally," or would the context influence our behavior and lead us to behave "abnormally"?

Phil Zimbardo conducted a seminal and provocative study to answer this question.[48] As the first step in what became known as the Stanford Prison study, Zimbardo first divided his young, healthy, intelligent participants into two groups: prisoners and guards, giving each group an appropriate uniform. The prisoners were placed in a makeshift prison, and the guards were simply instructed to keep order. The researchers were surprised to find they had to stop the study after only five days (they had expected to run it for several weeks), because the guards were mistreating the prisoners. The context of the prison and the role of prison guard proved to be unexpectedly powerful; the young, healthy, intelligent participants playing the role of prison guards "could not help" abusing the prisoners, and most of the prisoners conformed with the role of victims, some of them even becoming depressed and withdrawn. Zimbardo's study is important because it shows that total institutions can lead normal, healthy, intelligent people to behave in ways that one could validly label as abnormal and even destructive and "extremist."

An Important Lesson from Research on Conformity: "Normal" Individuals Can Become Abnormal and Even Extremist through the Influence of Group Norms

Terrorist groups are in *some* respects different and very unlike anything most people experience, but we must avoid thinking of terrorist groups as "alien" and as completely different from the kinds of groups we belong to in our everyday lives. Particularly in terms of how individual behavior is shaped by group norms, terrorist groups are like most other groups, even "ordinary" groups we belong to. The following are some basic features of norms that evolve in groups:

1. Arbitrary and incorrect group norms can influence behavior in major ways.
2. Group norms can deviate from the norms of mainstream society and become extremist.
3. The intelligence of individual group members will not necessarily serve to protect the group from adopting extremist and incorrect norms.
4. Radical members can influence group norms to become more extremist, even though individual members recognize the group is heading in the wrong direction.
5. Once established, group norms become an "independent" powerful force, a force that is "in the air" but not easy to grasp, an invisible molder of behavior; a force that is not easy to control by individual group members.

A number of well conceived studies in Western contexts demonstrate how even the most carefully planned groups, with "elite" members chosen for their efficiency and intelligence, can go down the wrong path as destructive norms evolve. Perhaps the most famous example is the research of Irving Janis on *groupthink*, the tendency for people in groups to converge on unwise courses of action they would have avoided if they were making the decision individually.[49] The focus of Janis's research was highly intelligent groups of decision-making elite in the U.S. government, who collectively made disastrous decisions in failing to prepare for a Japanese attack at Pearl Harbor during World War Two, thought up the failed Bay of Pigs invasion in Cuba in 1961, and escalated the war in Vietnam in the 1960s. To this list we could add more recent disastrous decisions made by groups of highly intelligent officials, such as the failure of intelligence prior to the tragedy of September 11, and the catastrophic "planning" for postinvasion Iraq.

Such cases demonstrate how groups of intelligent individuals can end up making disastrous decisions. A common key feature of such group situations, and one shared by terrorist groups, is secrecy. When groups "close up" and immune themselves from outside criticism, the probability of incorrect decisions substantially increase. This is not just because of a strong or authoritarian leader, but because of the power of group established norms.

OBEDIENCE AND TERRORIST GROUPS

"Blind obedience" is an idea that comes immediately to mind in association with terrorism, and particularly suicide terrorism. Images of the September 11 terrorists slamming planes full of passengers into skyscrapers filled with people, of suicide bombers in Iraq who strap themselves into cars loaded with explosives and obey orders to kill Iraqis and Americans alike . . . the global media is filled with such images in the first part of the twenty-first century. Why do these terrorists follow orders to destroy life, when to the rest of us it is clear that such orders should be disobeyed, no matter who issues them? Surely it is something about the individual terrorists that leads to such high levels of obedience to authority? Are they pathological? What would normal people like you and I do in such extraordinary circumstances? Would any of us be influenced by the situation to behave abnormally and to harm others?

"I am just an ordinary person, like you. If you had been there in my place, you would have done the same and followed orders. You would not have disobeyed." These words have often been spoken in their own defense by those who took part in mass murder and other crimes against humanity. They were spoken in trials at The Hague, when Nazi war criminals were brought to justice following World War II, and they have been spoken in many other courts of justice, including in trials held during the Vietnam war, the Bosnian conflict, and during the Iraq war. Typically, the criminal justice system has refused to accept this line of defense and insisted that at least some individuals be held responsible and not be allowed to use the excuse that "under the same circumstances any normal person would have done as I did and obeyed orders." The verdict in the trial of Private Lynndie England and others who were found guilty of mistreating Iraqi prisoners at the infamous Abu Ghraib prison attests to this.

But what if we were to set up an extraordinary situation in which an authority figure orders a "normal" person, like you and I, to harm others? Let us imagine carrying out the following experiment at a major university. First, a sample of males aged between twenty and fifty from different backgrounds is recruited to take part in a study (ostensibly) on learning. When a participant arrives at the laboratory, he is introduced to a second participant, a mild mannered middle-aged man, who is actually a confederate of the Experimenter. A coin is tossed to decide which of the two will be the teacher and which one will act as the learner in this "learning" experiment. The confederate always ends up playing the part of the learner and the "naive" participant always serves as the teacher.

The task of the teacher is to teach the learner word associations. For example, when the teacher says "sky," the learner should say "blue." Each time the student makes a mistake, the teacher has to punish the student. Punishment is administered using a "shock generator." On the shock generator machine, there are clear gradations going up in 15-volt intervals, from 0 to 450 volts. There are also labels on higher voltages, from "slight shock," "moderate shock," and "strong shock" all the way up to "danger," "danger: severe shock," and "XXX." The teacher is trained to use the shock generator, and receives a sample shock of

45 volts in order to make sure he understands the kind of pain involved in the punishments he might administer.

Each time the student makes a mistake, the teacher has to increase the shock level another 15 volts. If the teacher hesitates, the scientist running the experiment tells him, "Please continue." If the teacher still does not shock the student using the appropriate shock level, the scientist says, "You have no other choice, you must go on."

The research question is this: will the naive participants obey orders to shock the students at increasingly high levels, until they reach voltage levels that are clearly harmful and even fatal? This question was posed by the psychologist Stanley Milgram to a group of researchers, as well as to a group of lay people.[50] Milgram described the above experiment to both groups of researchers and lay people, and both groups predicted that participants, who had been identified through psychological testing as being "normal," would refuse to obey orders to give high levels of shock to the learner. They were proved to be wrong.

The results of the Milgram experiments on obedience to authority were a complete surprise and shocking to many people. About 60 percent of the participants, screened to fit the profile of normal personalities, gave dangerously high levels of shock to the learner. Of course, the experimental situation was rigged so that the learner only appeared to receive shocks and to suffer. In practice, the learner was acting out the part of someone receiving electric shock. But postexperimental interviews showed that participants found the learner's acting convincing and the experimental situation highly involving.

From cases such as that of Private Lynndie England, a female member of the U.S. military who was photographed holding a naked Iraqi prisoner at the end of a dog leash at Abu Ghraib prison, you will not be surprised to learn that women were found to behave very similar to men in the context of the Milgram obedience to authority experiment. The power of the situation and the authority of the scientist seemed to be too much for most women and men to resist.

But Milgram's studies also showed some ways in which obedience levels could be decreased. For example, the teacher was less likely to obey and to give a high level of shock to the learner when there were two authority figures present and they disagreed with one another about what the teacher should do. Also, the greater the distance between the teacher and the learner, the more likely was the teacher to administer high levels of shock. It was almost as if when the learner was out of sight, the learner's (assumed) suffering was out of mind as far as the teacher was concerned.

Why did so many people, including experts and lay people, react so strongly and negatively to the results of the Milgram studies on obedience to authority? These results were discussed in both the popular media and in the scientific community, with people taking strong positions for and against Milgram. The attacks on Milgram were in large part a reaction against the demonstration his research seemed to provide for the tremendous power of context to influence human behavior. Critics could not accept the implication that under certain conditions, normal people would behave in "abnormal" ways and potentially inflict extreme harm on others.

Of course, the Milgram experiments do not negate the idea that human beings enjoy some measure of free will and can intentionally choose between different courses of action.[51] The focus of discussions has typically been on the majority of naive participants acting as teachers who obeyed the authority figure and proceeded to do harm to the learner. However, from the point of view of democracy and the survival of an open society, far more important are the participants who refused to obey and refused to give the learner higher levels of electric shocks. The refusal of this minority to obey, and their intentional choice to take an alternative path, shows that although the power of the context is great, it can be overcome.

Degrees of Freedom and Individual "Free Will"

Research on conformity and obedience demonstrates that the context can have a crushing impact on individuals, reducing the degrees of freedom they have for making choices in behavior. Certain contexts reduce degrees of freedom so much that even normal people, with just a few of exceptions, choose to take actions that harm others.

The fact that most people choose to harm others in the context of the Milgram experiment does not mean that free will is nonexistent in such a context, but it does mean that selecting *not* to harm others in this context is a difficult choice to make. The powerful force of context in the Milgram experiment is pushing individuals to obey the authority figure and give higher levels of shock to the student, but some participants decide to resist this force. They feel uncomfortable resisting the authority figure, their anxiety level rises when they repeatedly refuse to obey, but resist and disobey they do; this is their choice and they leave the situation feeling that they made the right decision.

Similarly, in the conformity experiments of Sherif, Asch, Zimbardo, and others, the power of the context leads many, and often most, participants to choose to conform to prevailing norms. In Sherif's study, the norms in question are group-established norms about how much a spot of light moves (although it never actually moves); in Asch's experiments they are majority established norms about which of three lines is the same as a standard line (the majority makes the wrong choice), and in Zimbardo's simulation the norms are institutional and related to the roles of prison guards and prisoners (the roles are dysfunctional and lead to violence against others). But in each context, some participants choose to go against prevailing norms and to behave according to alternative, healthier norms.

Implications for Understanding Terrorism

Research on conformity and obedience clearly demonstrates that context has an overwhelming impact on how most of us behave, and under some conditions contextual pressures can lead at least some of us "normal" people to become utterly destructive and harmful. Authority figures and prevailing norms are of paramount importance in shaping behavior. In some communities, what we call "terrorism" is seen as a legitimate and rational strategy for fighting against "barbarian invaders." It is in this light that we can better understand suicide terrorism.

SUICIDE TERRORISTS AS THE POOR ARMY'S GUIDED MISSILES

Perhaps the aspect of terrorism that has been least well understood by Western commentators is suicide terrorism. The major reason for mis-understandings is the assumption that the best explanation for suicide terrorism focuses on the characteristics of the individual suicide terrorist. Surely the suicide terrorist must be insane, idiotic, illiterate, psychologically abnormal, and completely different from the rest of us. This focus on individual characteristics, and neglect of context, is utterly mistaken and misleading.

We need to understand suicide terrorism in the larger context of a perceived war, in which a smaller, weaker, ill-equipped army fights a much stronger army. In order to clarify this point, I begin by highlighting the strategic use of suicide terrorism by military forces with few resources and then briefly reviewing the recent history of suicide terrorism.

Suicide terrorism is a rational strategy adopted by fighting groups with relatively few resources at war with a much more powerful adversary. Suicide terrorists are the guided missiles of poor armies; they are the equivalent of what the U.S. military has in terms of satellite guidance systems and the precision missiles they direct at specific targets. Suicide terrorists can also hit their targets with pinpoint accuracy, using human intelligence and human lives as the main resource.

What makes suicide terrorism strategically so effective is that it is very difficult, in practice perhaps impossible, to guard against. Modern economies rely on mass movements of people, particularly in and around major urban centers housing tens of millions of people from different ethnic, religious, and national backgrounds. The diversity of people moving across borders and in and out of major urban centers makes it even more difficult to screen for suicide terrorists. The July 2005 suicide bombings in London illustrate this point: the four "home grown" suicide terrorists were part of immigrant communities settled in England, but had ties to radicals in Pakistan. In essence, these were "terrorists without borders" putting into effect a rational plan for bringing the London transportation system and economy to a standstill.

Of course, to say that an action is rational is not to justify that action; it is simply to point out that the action does not arise from irrational forces or some kind of "craziness." Obviously suicide terrorism breaches the Geneva Conventions, most importantly by targeting civilians (critics of the United States would argue that the administration of President George W. Bush has also willfully set aside the Geneva Conventions during the invasion and occupation of Iraq).

A second point, distinct from the issue of rationality, is that in terms of its history in modern times, suicide terrorism is not necessarily tied to religion, it was first used extensively by secular, nationalist forces. The use of grenade-strapped foot soldiers against machine gun positions in trench warfare during World War I (1914–1918) was an early example of a "suicide mission," because the attackers were often killed. The Japanese military used so-called "kamikaze pilots" to try to destroy U.S. and allied ships: these were basically missiles guided by suicide pilots into enemy targets (rather like a suicide car bomber directing his vehicle to explode against a U.S.-armored vehicle in occupied Iraq). But the modern history of suicide terrorism really begins with the Tamil Tigers in Sri Lanka, who in their fight for independence for the Tamil minority carried out hundreds of suicide attacks against government targets.

The Tamil Tigers represent an ethnic independence movement, not a religious movement. The special group of suicide terrorists they trained, the so-called Black Tigers, were a strategic force against the much larger and better equipped government forces. The motivation of the Black Tigers was to achieve an independent Tamil homeland; they were not motivated by religious zeal. In his book *Dying to Win: The Strategic Logic of Suicide Terrorism*, Robert Pape has pointed out that in the 1980s and 1990s, through until 2002 when the Tamil Tigers agreed to a cease-fire with the Sri Lankan government, the Tigers accounted for about a quarter of all suicide attacks committed around the world.[52]

The last decades of the twentieth century saw a rise in Islamic suicide terrorism. These include suicide attacks by Chechen Muslims against Russian interests, and by Al Qaeda mainly against the United States and its allies. The largest of these attacks was the tragedy of September 11, and since then the focus has shifted to Iraq. Of course, the reasons why Al Qaeda and other radical Islamic forces attack Russian, U.S., and other majority group interests around the world have religious roots. But the same goal of "freeing Islamic lands" from non-Muslim forces could be attempted through many strategies other than suicide bombings.

There is nothing inherent to Islam that leads radical Muslims to adopt suicide terrorism. However, there is something characteristic of radical Muslims as a minority confronted by overwhelming enemy forces that is shared by some other minorities, such as Tamils in Sri Lanka faced by overwhelming government forces, which leads them to adopt suicide terrorism as a rational strategic choice. For example, in postwar Iraq, approximately 15,000 lightly armed and poorly trained insurgents are fighting a relatively far better equipped and superbly trained force of about 150,000 U.S. soldiers, as well as tens of thousands of U.S. military contractors and forces from the United Kingdom, Italy, Australia, Poland, and other nations. The insurgents are outnumbered, outgunned, and out-trained, in every way.

Suicide terrorism provides the insurgents with an unpredictable and unstoppable lethal weapon that the other side does not have.

From the terrorists' point of view, suicide terrorism is highly effective in part because it attracts enormous worldwide media attention. Estimates of the number of Iraqi civilian deaths since the start of the Iraq invasion in March 2003 vary from around 20,000 (as estimated by the group *Iraq Body Count*, in July 2005) to 30,000 (as estimated by President G.W. Bush in December 2005), to 100,000 (published in the British medical journal *The Lancet*, in October 2004). Although American fire is responsible for the largest number of Iraqi civilians killed (even "precision bombing" results in horrendous civilian casualties), it is civilian death by suicide terrorism that has attracted by far the highest level of media attention. It is a bizarre accident of war that both terrorist groups and the U.S. government would rather keep the media focus on the (relatively smaller) casualties resulting from suicide bombings.

American generals have declared "we don't do body counts," but the world media does do body counts, and it is to the world media that suicide terrorists are speaking.

Much has been made in the media of the money and favorable recognition received by the families of some suicide terrorists in some parts of the world, with the implication that suicide terrorism would end if monetary rewards were cut off. For example the former Iraqi dictator Saddam Hussein's Baath Party reportedly sent the families of suicide terrorists in the West Bank $15,000 each. But it would be far too simplistic to suppose that we can end suicide terrorism by rooting out the monetary reward system that supposedly feeds the fire of suicide terrorism. The family of the four suicide bombers who struck London in July 2005 did not receive monetary rewards or mass media adulation—quite the reverse. Similarly, the families of the hundreds of suicide terrorists who have struck in postwar Iraq did not profit momentarily; many of them remain anonymous in death. Although monetary rewards can have an influence on suicide terrorism, they do not play the vitally important causal role often assumed.

CHAPTER 10

Contextualized Democracy as a Solution to Terrorism

"More troops! That's the solution to defeating terrorism."
"Improved technology! The war on terror can only be won by better technology."
"Profiling! Terrorists are sick, abnormal individuals, and we can defeat them by identifying and exterminating them one by one."
"Better human intelligence! The best way to win the war on terror is to improve covert operations in societies that produce terrorists."

More troops, improved technology, more effective profiling, better human intelligence—these have been the dominant policy responses to global terror. Although all of these can be part of a solution to terrorism, they will never win the war on terror because such policies only target those *individuals whose identities have already been transformed and who have already reached* the highest floors on the staircase to terrorism. Such policies are reductionist, because they see the solution to be the identification of individual terrorists. Such policies have not worked, because they neglect the most important floors on the staircase, the first few floors where the vast majority of the population exists.

The primary policy implication of the staircase metaphor is familiar to professionals researching and practicing in health care: prevention is the long-term solution to terrorism. We must think long-term rather than short-term, proactive rather than reactive, societal and not individualistic. In essence, we must shift to prevention as a global response to terrorism.

But why should we expect prevention to work in the realm of terrorism, when it has not been implemented in other domains? Why should we expect politicians and decision makers to "change their spots" now and dedicate themselves to prevention? The answer is clear: because we no longer have a choice. The costs of continuing the current individualistic, reactive policies are too great. Western democracies cannot afford the economic, political, and social costs of more tragedies on the scale of September 11. There is no choice but to change from a reactive to a proactive policy, and to take up prevention by looking to the ground floor conditions that ultimately give rise to terrorism on the highest floor of the staircase.

Research on conformity, obedience, and the power of context clearly demonstrates that under certain conditions, some individuals will inevitably climb up from the ground floor, adopt a morality condoning terrorism, identify with terrorist groups, and wind their way up the staircase to commit acts of terror. Although certain individuals are more likely than others to become terrorists, it would be an enormous mistake to base policy on identifying profiles of "potential terrorists," or even the "extremists" who incite terrorism.

In every society, including Western democracies, there are present individuals and even groups who actively and publicly espouse vile, fanatical ideologies. Just about every variety of vile fanaticism can be found in the United States: from religious fascists to white supremacists, from antiglobalization extremists to one-world fanatics, every shade of extreme is present and often represented by no more than a handful, or sometimes even just one, exponent. With particular reference to religion, the same kinds of fascistic religious fundamentalists who are active in parts of the Islamic world can be identified in the Christian world, and indeed in the worlds of the other major religions.

The difference is that the twenty-first century context of the Islamic world has given rise to relatively widespread sympathy and even some active support for fanatical causes. We must ask what it is about the context and sociopolitical conditions of the Islamic world that has led to sympathy and even support for Islamic fascists, whereas Christian fascists garner relatively less sympathy and support from the general public of their societies. Our focus, then, must remain on the material and cultural context, conditions on the ground floor.

It is conditions on the ground floor that lead to terrorism. As long as conditions remain the same, removing one set of individuals at the top of the staircase to terrorism will only make room for another set to step forward and take their place. We must attend to the context, the general conditions that give rise to terrorism. Only by reforming conditions on the ground floor can we prevent individuals from climbing to the top of the staircase and carrying out terrorist acts. Such a policy shift toward prevention may appear risky, but in practice it provides the best long-term safeguard against terrorism.

But how can conditions on the ground floor be altered in a constructive way? In the search for solutions, a great deal has been said about "democracy" and the creation of civil societies, but how can this be achieved? At the same time that we hear talk of democracy for the third world, we hear dire warnings about the consequences of "exporting democracy." The major problem in postwar Iraq, critics claim, is that we have attempted to export American-style democracy to a country with a very different culture. This seems to leave the United States and other Western powers in a "damned if you do, and damned if you don't" predicament. If they try to introduce democracy, they are accused of cultural insensitivity, and if they do not try to introduce democracy, they are accused of supporting the dictatorship and the status quo.

Is there a way of supporting more openness in third world societies, without "exporting democracy" in a way that backfires and has destructive consequences? I believe there is, and to illustrate some possibilities I discuss an example of *contextualized democracy,* the use of local cultural symbols and meaning systems as a way of strengthening democratic trends and bringing into place a democratic state.

But before I discuss contextualized democracy, I need to stress two points. First, a preventive policy does not imply that we abandon short-term programs for fighting those who have climbed the staircase to terrorism and are already active terrorists. I see a need for long-term, context oriented solutions to go hand-in-hand with short-term strategies to deal with the small number of individuals who have already climbed up to the top of the staircase and are active terrorists.

Second, contextualized democracy does not mean that we take a relativist approach and abandon the idea that certain basic rights, freedoms, and duties have to be present in order for a society to be counted as a democracy, irrespective of the religion(s), language(s), and other characteristics of that society. For example, the principle of equal treatment before the law should not be abandoned.

The "rule of law" is perhaps the most important, foundational step toward democracy. Even in conditions where the law gives different groups of people different rights and duties, the idea that every person will be treated according to the law must be adhered to as a starting point on the road to democracy.

A second step is to change laws so that everyone is afforded the same basic rights and duties. This will be particularly challenging in the Near and Middle East, but it is a step that will eventually have to be taken. This will require changes in laws pertaining to women. I see this as a particularly important point, because I am convinced that effective and foundational policies to end terrorism must involve transformations in the identity, and thus role, of women in societies that nurture moralities supportive of terrorism.

THE PSYCHOLOGICAL CITIZEN, SHI'A ISLAM, AND CONTEXTUALIZED DEMOCRACY

Each type of economic–political system, whether it be democratic or dictatorial, capitalist or socialist, religious or secular, requires its citizens to have particular psychological characteristics in order for the system to function and survive. Citizens must have the kinds of psychological characteristics that match the requirements of the economic–political system. If a "good fit" is not achieved, then the economic–political system will collapse, sooner or later.

Consider, for example, the experiences of the former Soviet Union. The 1917 revolution in Russia eventually led to the end of the rule of the Tzars and the establishment of a communist state. The new economic-political system of the U.S.S.R. brought an end to major forms of private property, and initiated collective farming, state ownership of industry, and other such historic changes. This new system required transformed psychological citizens to make it a success; for example, it required psychological citizens who would be motivated to work hard even when the rewards of their extra efforts did not go directly to them personally. Of course, it also required leaders who would not take personal advantage of their higher status and power. But neither leaders nor the ordinary citizens in the Soviet system changed enough to make the new economic–political system work effectively, and this was an important factor resulting in the collapse of the Soviet empire by the early 1980s.

The maximum speed of change is always faster at the macrolevel of economic and political systems than it is at the microlevel of psychological characteristics of people. This relationship has been referred to as a macro/micro universal law of change.[53] Governments, economic policies, and the "laws of the land" can change almost overnight, but changing the psychological characteristics of a population requires a far longer time. This difference between the maximum speed of change at macro economic–political–legal levels and the micropsychological level is in part responsible for the much discussed "paradox of revolution;" even after major revolutions, observers begin to notice that in many ways nothing has really changed. Alphonse Karr made his famous observation *Plus ça change, plus c'est le même chose* (The more things change, the more they stay the same) in reference to revolutions.

The psychological citizen, then, serves as the foundation for any economic–political system.[54] If the foundation cannot support the building on top, the entire edifice will eventually collapse. The most important features of the psychological citizen can be better recognized through identifying subtypes:

The developmental citizen: The psychological growth of the child toward the goal of comprehending and eventually playing an active role in the economic–political order.

The cognitive citizen: The mental skills required by adults to achieve adequate comprehension, evaluation, and to make choices in the economic–political system.

The social citizen: The social skills required by adults to make the appropriate choices and interventions in the economic–political system.

The developmental, cognitive, and social requirements for success are very different across different types of economic–political systems. For example, in a democracy, characteristics are needed that will mold active rather than bystander citizens. But not all democracies are the same, even within Western societies (this point is further discussed later in this Chapter). Differences across democracies are in large part due to the cultural and historic foundations of particular societies.

Just as established Western democracies differ in major ways in line with each of their unique cultures, new democracies should also be adapted to the cultural contexts of each society. The idea of contextualized democracy suggests that democracy in Iraq need not and should not be in every major way the same as democracy in the United States or other Western societies.

The idea of contextualized democracy is encapsulated in the following four propositions:

1. The successful implementation of democracy (as well as other political systems) and its manifestation in everyday life is to a considerable degree dependent on local cultural characteristics.
2. Some local cultural characteristics are neutral, some are detrimental, and others are supportive of democracy.
3. When local cultural characteristics supportive of democracy can be appropriated, adapted, and utilized, democracy will grow on firmer ground.
4. By developing democracy through fusion with local cultural characteristics supportive of democracy, it will be more feasible to overcome local cultural characteristics opposed to democracy.

I will use the example of Shi'a Islam to further clarify the potential of contextualized democracy and show how they play out in practice. I have selected Shi'a Islam because of the dominant importance of Shi'a Islam in the political future of Iraq, and the importance of Iraq in the so-called war on terror and the establishment of democracy in the Near and Middle East.

Shi'a Islam: Historical Background and Contemporary Scene

The launching of Islam as a religious, cultural, and political, movement in the seventh century was associated with a number of fragmentations within the Islamic world. The most significant split to occur involved the birth of Shi'a Islam, which today is the largest and most vibrant "minority" group outside the "majority" group of Sunni Islam. The beginnings of Shi'a Islam are rooted in conflicts over the succession of leadership after the death of the Prophet Muhammad in 632; the Prophet did not have living sons and according to many Muslims did not appoint a successor.

Shi'a Muslims believe that the legitimate successor to the Prophet was his closest and ablest relative, his cousin and son-in-law Ali. But Ali had to wait until after the periods of leadership of three of the Prophets companions, before he was finally selected as Caliph in 656. However, oppositions factions, led by the Prophet Muhammad's wife A'isha, forced Ali from power and he was stabbed to death in 661. His sons, Hassan and Hussein, continued to fight for what they believed to be their right to succession to the caliphate, but they were defeated by overwhelming forces. The martyrdom of Hussein and his small band of followers at Karbala, Iraq, in 680, is traditionally seen as the launching pad for Shi'a Islam. After this, Shi'a Islam would always be the most important minority branch of Islam, akin to the Protestant Church having branched away to form another brand of Christianity.

Today Shi'a Islam is practiced by about 96 percent of the population of Iran, and about 60 percent of the population of Iraq.

Democracy and Culture

Democracy has its roots in the culture of the Greek city states of 2,500 years ago, where it meant rule by the *demos*, the citizens. Because of the small size of the individual Greek states and the small number of individuals who qualified as citizens within each state, it was possible to practice *direct democracy*, meaning that citizens could personally participate in debates and decision making. But the enormous size of the modern state and its citizenry has necessitated *indirect democracy*, meaning that citizens elect representatives who participate in decision making on their behalf.

There are enormous variations in the way that modern states put democracy into practice. For example, one form of variation concerns the *electoral system*, the way in which the votes of citizens for candidates are converted to seats for offices. The United Kingdom and most former colonies of the British Empire, including the United States, India, and Canada use plurality rule, meaning that the candidates with the most votes win the seats. This often means that the governing party has less than majority support among the voting population. But most Western European democracies (with the exception of the United Kingdom) use proportional representation, meaning that the representation of a political party in the country's assemblies (senate, parliament, and so on) is proportional to the votes they receive. Various forms of majoritarian rule also exist, such as in Australia and France, where a candidate must win the majority of votes in order to be elected.

Not only do democracies differ to the degree that they are plurality rule, proportional, or majoritarian in their electoral systems, but they differ in how they implement these different systems. For example, plurality rule democracies differ as to how the head of the legislative branch of government (i.e., the prime minister, president, and so on) is selected. In the United Kingdom, it is the leader of the party with the majority of members in parliament; in the United States, it is the person who receives most votes from the Electoral College. In the U.K. system, the Prime Minister is necessarily leader of the ruling party. In the United States, the President can be from a party that has minority status in the House of Representatives and the Senate.

Another example of how democracies differ concerns the power of minorities to block legislation. For example, in the U.S. Senate a minority party can block legislation if it can get over 40 percent of the senate votes. In Switzerland, on some issues much smaller cantons can block legislation that affect the entire nation, in a system that is often described as involving a "double democracy."

My goal here is not to conduct a wide survey of different types of procedures used by states to implement democracy, but to cite selective examples to demonstrate that basically the same democratic ideals are being brought to fruition through sometimes very different procedures. The exact ways in which democracy is implemented vary in important ways across cultures. But a fundamental question arises at this point: what exactly are the key features of democracy that should remain consistent, which must be present, irrespective of the cultural context?

Psychological research suggests that a key feature, perhaps the most important, that must be present if a political system is to be accepted as a democracy is that citizens feel they are included in decision making and their voice matters.[55] Irrespective of the outcome, people feel that they have been treated more fairly if they believe they have been engaged in the procedures leading to decision making. Of course, people do not feel that their voice matters in a situation where the vast majority of them are utterly dissatisfied with the leadership of their society, but they are not able to replace the leadership.

In the context of the Near and Middle East (and other nondemocratic regions of the world), the most fundamental democratic right is the right of the people to vote political leaders *out* of office, and to replace them with candidates of their own choosing. Elections are already routinely held in a number of Near and Middle Eastern countries, including the larger ones such as Egypt, Iran, and Pakistan, but such elections are not democratic because the people are not allowed to vote political leaders out of office and replace them with "unvetted" candidates. The end result is that the vast majority of people do not feel that they are involved in the decision-making process, despite being coerced to "cast their votes."

Of course, there are many alternative practical avenues through which it is possible to achieve this broad goal of getting people to feel that they are part of the decision-making process.[56] Examples can include:

- developing mechanisms to make the government accountable for its actions;
- developing an independent judiciary;
- developing grassroots participation, where citizens openly exchange opinions and information in "town hall" meetings.

But what is the relationship between these "practical avenues" and political elections? From one perspective, accountability, an independent judiciary, and grassroots participation are prerequisites for free and fair political elections; they are what lead to free and fair elections. Second, because it is not possible to export accountability, an independent judiciary, and grassroots participation, "exporting democracy" is not a viable option. From this viewpoint, when we attempt to "export democracy," all we end up exporting are elections, which in practice turn into the types of elections already in place in dictatorships such as Cuba and Iran.

Free and fair elections are seen, then, as the end result, rather than the starting point, of growth toward a democratic system. When elections are introduced to a country without a history of accountability, an independent judiciary, and grassroots participation, the result is a procedure so flawed that to call it a democratic election is to distort the idea of democratic elections beyond recognition. It would be like expecting a fair sentence from a judge when all that preceded her judgment, including defense and prosecution lawyers arguing cases, witnesses giving evidence, and juries deliberating, was completely wrong or missing from the procedures.

Should we wait for accountability, an independent judiciary, and grassroots participation to evolve and then lead to free and fair elections in countries such as Iraq? Or, is it better to "export" elections, in whatever shape possible, and then work backward to try to develop the political culture and systems needed to support free and fair elections? The answer to these questions depends a great deal on the quality of management achieved. For example, in the case of Iraq, if postwar developments had been well managed, then introducing elections first and then trying to build the democratic culture to support elections would have been more feasible. But the poor management of postwar events in Iraq has made it far more difficult to "make democracy work," moving backward from elections.

Cultural Characteristics: Neutral, Detrimental, and Supportive of Democracy

Within each of the many countries that presently do not enjoy a democratic system, there are cultural characteristics that are neutral toward democracy, meaning they do not oppose or support democratic tendencies. For example, the fact that poetry and calligraphy achieve an extraordinarily high standard in Islamic culture is neutral to the practice of democracy. Some other characteristics are detrimental, in that they actively oppose democratic tendencies. For example, the strictly hierarchical and male-dominated tribal system of Saudi Arabia and a number of other key Islamic societies is detrimental to democratic movements in the region. Still others are supportive of democracies. For example, the traditional relationship between clergy and the people in Shi'a Iran and Iraq is potentially supportive of democracy, as I explain below, starting my explanation with questions about democratic movements in the region.

Consider the following question: how is it that since the end of the nineteenth century, as the idea of democracy spread around the world and eventually reached Near and Middle-Eastern communities, the opposition to the various dictatorial Persian Shahs, first of the Qajar dynasty and then the Pahlavi dynasty, was led by Shi'a clergy (*rohaniyat*)? Why is it that the collective movements against the dictatorship of Saddam Hussein in Iraq found their voice in the leadership of clergy like Ayatollah Sadre? This seems unexpected, given the conservative and "undemocratic" image of Shi'a Islam that is found in the Western media. In order to better address these issues, we need to look closely at the development of Shi'a clergy and at the relationship between Shi'a clergy and the people in their societies

In particular, we must consider the situation of Shi'a clergy in Iran, after the "Twelver" Shi'a movement came to dominate society with the dawn of the Safavi Dynasty in 1501 (these Shi'a are known as the "Twelvers" because they follow the twelve Imams who were the descendants of Ali, rather than the caliphs followed by Sunni Muslims).

The dependency of the Shi'a clergy on the State lessened toward the end of the Safavi Dynasty, and by 1722 when the last Safavi ruler was overthrown some of the important Shi'a clergy had moved to Najaf and other holy cities in Iraq (then under Ottoman control). The move to Ottoman Iraq means that Iranian Shi'a clergy were out of the control of the rulers in Iran (just as in his eventually successful struggle against the last of the Pahlavi Dynasty, Ayatollah Khomeini moved to Iraq and then briefly to France, before his triumphant return with the 1978–1979 revolution).

In the late eighteenth and during the nineteenth century, three developments took place in Shi'a Islam that would profoundly impact the role of the clergy and the relationship between the clergy and the people.

First, the clergy gradually developed economic independence from the government, by taking Islamic taxes directly from the faithful and also by building up Islamic charities and funds, which they in turn used to extend their influence in Shi'a communities, local, national, and international. The tradition emerged that each of the faithful would donate their Islamic taxes to a clergy of their personal choice.

In practical terms, this led to greater independence of the clergy from government authorities, but far greater dependency of the clergy on their followers. Eventually, Shi'a clergy became almost completely dependent on followers to provide them with an income through Islamic taxes. This translated into very close ties between the clergy and the faithful: if I am going to persuade you to pay religious taxes to me voluntarily, then I had better have good communications with you and attend closely to your needs and priorities. If I fail, you could give your Islamic taxes to another cleric, or not give them at all.

The key feature of this new financial arrangement between the clergy and the faithful was that each Shi'a individual could freely choose to support particular clergy from a number of different "candidates" seeking support. This choice was not present in the relationship between individual citizens and the central government in Iran, because citizens were forced to pay taxes to the one and only Shah irrespective of their own inclinations.

A second parallel development was the idea that each Shi'a Muslim must select a worthy cleric as a source of imitation (*marja-i-taqlid*), a person who would clarify how all the various choices in life should be made (including by publishing detailed guidelines, as explained later in this Chapter). There could be a number of sources of imitation, and typically the most important ones would be located near the holy sights of Shi'a Islam, particularly Najaf, Karbala, and Kazimayn in Iraq. By the end of the nineteenth century, a tradition emerged that a few, or sometimes just one, source of imitation would be recognized by most of the Shi'a faithful as a supreme leader. In the nineteenth and much of the twentieth century (prior to the 1978–79 revolution in Iran), the *marja-i-taqlid* was not just a spiritual source of inspiration but also, and at times more importantly, an authority *independent* of the government.

A third development in Shi'a Islam that enabled the Shi'a clergy to play a vital role in leading the reform and revolutionary movements of the nineteenth and twentieth century was the gradual transformation and centralization of clerical authority. These developments took place in association with the growth of religious training seminaries (*howzeh*) around major Shi'a shrine centers. Theology students (*talabeh*) would attend lectures and seminars and, depending on their abilities and motivations, become recognized to have attained different levels of expertise and competence in a number of study areas, particularly jurisprudence and its fundamental principles (*fiqh va usul*), as well as spiritual philosophy (*irfan*). Through participation in classes, debates, and also through working with people outside seminaries, students could become recognized as having attained the rank of *Hojjatoleslam*, and a much smaller number would progress to eventually be recognized as *ayatollahs*.

It is often said that "Islam has no Pope," but this statement is not strictly accurate, in Shi'a Islam at least. During the last century, there have emerged Ayatollahs who have enjoyed a leadership status similar to that of the Pope in the Catholic Church. Indeed, as I discuss in the next section, a strong argument could be made for the case that leadership in Shi'a Islam is far more democratic and in touch with the masses than leadership in the Christian church.

THREE "DEMOCRATIC" SHI'A TRADITIONS

Three central "democratic" features of the traditional Shi'a seminary system, such as the most important Iranian seminary situated in Ghom (*howzeh elmieh Ghom*), are (1) the collective and participatory nature of decision making (2) the relative freedom of students to attend different classes and meetings, and (3) the financial independence of the seminary. Each of these points warrants and deserves clarification.

(1) Clerical Titles by Consensus and Popular Support

The title attained by an individual in the traditional Shi'a clerical system arises out of collective consensus, and is not "given" by a single authority. For example, after some years of study and participation in the life of a seminary, as well as service in mosques and centers outside the seminary, a student (*talabeh*) might be recognized as a *Hojjatoleslam*. Such recognition would come from his superiors, as well as his peers. Because his superiors are not part of a rigid hierarchy and are not all located in one place, some would come to know the aspirant by his reputation.

As an aspiring and successful *Hojjatoleslam* gains more and more experience, he would typically teach and gather students and followers. He would attract larger audiences at his sermons, but he would also publish and gain a still wider audience through his writings. Eventually, he may become recognized as an ayatollah. Those who attain this status gain the right and authority for interpretation (*ijtihad*) of spiritual and worldly matters.

A few ayatollahs eventually become recognized as Grand Ayatollah (*ayatollah ozma*) and serve as a source of imitation for very large numbers of people, sometimes dispersed in many countries.

The last internationally accepted *marja-i-taqlid* who remained untainted by the politics of regimes in Iran and Iraq was the Iranian-born Grand Ayatollah Khu'i (Abu al-Qasim al-Khu'i) who died in Iraq in 1992. As has become the custom for Grand Ayatollahs, he published a detailed guide (*risala*) for his followers, providing judgments and interpretations for behavior and decision making in their everyday lives. If one were to ask, "How did Khu'i become one of the two or three most important Grand Ayatollahs of his generation?" the answer would be that he attained this lofty stature through general consensus among Shi'a clergy and the Shi'a faithful, and not from any single governmental or nongovernmental authority.

But even at the height of his influence, Grand Ayatollah Khu'i could not dictate to other Shi'a ayatollahs or even to all the Shi'a faithful. In the tradition of Shi'a Islam, the geographical dispersion of important ayatollahs has been associated with the possibility of dissenting voices, or at least differences of opinion among leading clergy.

(2) Flexibility of Seminary Education

Shi'a seminaries (particularly prior to 1978) were in important respects like medieval universities in Europe: insular, informal, male, small, independent, and flexible in terms of the age at which students (*talabeh*) entered and how many years they continued their studies. The seminaries grew around important Shi'a Muslim shrines, and the learned men (*ulama*) who gathered there and served as teachers. There were no official entrance examinations for students seeking to study at seminaries, but the difficult years of study and austere living conditions served as an effective control on the number of students.

In the traditional Shi'a seminary system, students are free to seek out teachers and attend their classes and meetings. There is no formal examination and graduation system and no specifications about the number of years a student must study at the seminary; rather, peers and teachers guide students to classes and seminars that are appropriate for their personal level of attainment, as well as whether they have dedicated a sufficient number of years to a particular stage of their studies. Students rely on the seminary for rooming and a stipend, and if they are not making adequate progress they are not supported.

The relationship between student and teacher, for example a *talabeh* and an ayatollah teaching at a seminary, is to some degree shaped by the system of religious taxes in Shi'a Islam. The ayatollah is likely to be the recipient of Islamic taxes from some followers (*moghalledeen*), as well as to have influence over funds from some Islamic charities (*mowghoofeh*). If his student is performing well, the ayatollah can use Islamic taxes and charities to provide the student with financial support. I have been witness to an Ayatollah giving money to students who regularly attended his classes (no doubt students attending my lectures would like to get the same treatment). But I have also witnessed a seminary teacher adamantly refusing to give money to a rather unhappy *talabeh*, who had failed to attend classes regularly enough.

(3) Financial Independence of Seminaries

The Shi'a seminaries evolved to become financially independent, and this independence allowed for seminaries to evade government control and sometimes to oppose government policies. The sources of income for the seminaries were Islamic taxes (*khums*, *zakat*, *jizya*, and *kharaj*) given directly by the faithful, but also gifts of land and property, as well as additional monetary donations given by pilgrims visiting the holy Shi'a shrines around which seminaries were built.

Financial independence meant that government agencies found it far more difficult to control the curricula and teachings at seminaries. However, financial independence did not guarantee that the seminaries would not be attacked by central governments. For example, in March 1963 the Shah of Iran sent troops to attack and ransack the most important seminary in Ghom (*Madrasa Fayziya*), where Ayatollah Khomeini had been making speeches critical of the Shah's government. After a brief period of imprisonment in Iran and exile in Turkey, Khomeini made his way to Najaf and remained there from 1965 to 1978, where the seminaries and mosques were out of direct reach of the Shah and financially independent of the Iraqi regime centered in Baghdad.

THE CLERGY AND THE STATE IN POST-REVOLUTION IRAN AND POSTWAR IRAQ

The relative political and economic independence of the Shi'a clergy and the seminary system training them, allowed the clergy to take an oppositional stand to the Iranian government of the day in a number of decisive confrontations in the nineteenth and twentieth centuries. The most important examples are the opposition of the clergy to the Reuter concession in 1873, their opposition to the British tobacco monopoly in 1891–1892, and their participation in the movement to revise the constitution in 1905–1911. All these struggles were eventually won by the clergy: the Reuter concession was annulled, the British tobacco monopoly was ended, and although the constitutional movement victories of the early twentieth century was sidetracked and delayed until 1978 by the reign of the Pahlavi dynasty, the clergy did in the end achieve a complete victory over the Shah and the system of hereditary monarchy.

I want to emphasize that the independence of the Shi'a clergy from the ruling government made it possible for the clergy to play a critical, antidictatorship and often progressive role, while they remained "outsiders" and in opposition. The "antiestablishment" position of the Shi'a clergy was in practice vital to several major reform movements in modern Iranian history. As long as the Shi'a clergy were outside the government, despite reactionary elements within the clergy, there were some opportunities for the clergy to influence developments toward reform and progress.

Unfortunately, the influence of reactionary elements within the clergy meant that progress remained very limited, particularly in areas such as the full economic, legal, and political participation of women in Iranian society. Thus, the progressive role of Shi'a Islam in Iran has not just depended on the mosque remaining as an opposition force to the government, but also more progressive elements gaining greater influence in how Islam is interpreted.

But the 1978–1979 revolution in Iran completely changed the role of the "oppositional" clergy, because with the establishment of the Islamic Republic of Iran, the clergy had now become the government. Other Islamic leaders, including Sayyid Qutb in Egypt and Mawlana Mawdudi in India and Pakistan, had called for Islamic Republics earlier than Khomeini, but it was in Iran and through Khomeini's leadership that this goal was first realized in a modern state.

The establishment of the Islamic Republic brought to power Ayatollah Khomeini and a group of younger clergy who followed his radical interpretation of Islam. A central feature of this interpretation, as enshrined in the new Iranian constitution, is the principle of governance by a supreme religiously qualified leader (*velayat-e-faghih*) or, if one person is not recognized as clearly above others, then a small council of spiritual leaders. Khomeini served as the Supreme Leader (*vali faghih*) during his lifetime, and after him came Ali Khamene'i. The ascendance of Ali Khamene'i demonstrates how religious authority can be determined to a far higher degree than tradition warrants by political power in contemporary Iran.

Just as political favor led to the swift march of Khamene'i up to the ranks of ayatollah and spiritual leader, political disfavor led others to fall in ranks. For example, in 1979 Grand Ayatollah Kazem Shari'atmadari was put under house arrest and then "demoted" to a mere "mister," and Hussein Ali Montazeri was first given the title Grand Ayatollah and Khomeini's heir-apparent for four years, before he was removed and demoted to "mister" in March 1989.

The promotion of Khamene'i and others who followed Khomeini's line, and the demotion of Shari'atmadari and others who opposed Khomeini's line, clearly demonstrates that once the Shi'a clergy captured political power in Iran, the role of the clergy as critics of the government and as a possible avenue to a more open society had become very limited, and perhaps even ended. Formerly the clerics had been critics of government corruption, now they were part of it. Formerly the clerics had called for an end to the secret police, and to the imprisonment, torture, and assassination of political dissidents, now they were part of the government responsible for widespread violations of human rights.

Contextualized Democracy in Iran: A Hopeful Future?

From one perspective the future looks bleak for democracy in Iran, because a dictatorship by the Shah has been replaced by a dictatorship by the ayatollahs, the "turban for the crown" as one commentator aptly put it.[57] The "elections" held in Iran have become meaningless, because only vetted candidates who are part of the ruling system are permitted to run for office, and there is no free press to critically assess, and no independent judiciary to judge, those who do "win" political offices. Iran is a clear contemporary example of how elections can be turned into a tool for sustaining dictatorship. Coupled with repression within Iranian borders, the dictatorship in Iran has a history of supporting what the United States has designated as "terrorist groups," such as Hezbollah in Lebanon, and of assassinating numerous opposition figures abroad, including the former Prime Minister, Shahpour Bakhtiar, killed in France in 1991.

But from an alternative perspective there is realistic hope that democracy will eventually be strengthened in Iran, through a reformation in Shi'a Islam itself. The coming to power of Shi'a clergy is not only changing government in Iran, but it is also changing the Shi'a clergy. In the longer term, the seminaries and the education of Shi'a clergy is changing. The dawn of the twenty-first century sees Shi'a clergy in transition, and facing difficult alternative choices.

On the one hand, the seminaries are under pressure to give up financial autonomy and to become fully subservient to the government and the supreme leader (*vali faghih*). This would include subservience in the promotion of particular clerics to the ranks of ayatollahs and grand ayatollahs. On the other hand, there are strong factions within the clerical establishment who are determined to maintain the independence of the seminaries and the clerical system, and to ensure that the government does not interfere in the process of promotions (and demotions) of clerics. The possibility of democracy in Iran depends in large part on the outcome of these power struggles.

The subservience of the seminaries to government control will end the potential "reform" or "corrective" role that the mosque can have on government policies.

The Situation in Iraq

In Iraq, also, the Shi'a clergy had played an important historical role as leaders of the opposition to dictatorial rule centered in Baghdad. As in Iran, the central Iraqi government did not tolerate opposition political parties or any political voices of dissent, but no government had the power to close mosques. Individual clerics could be assassinated, as did happen to the Grand Ayatollah Mohammed Baqir al-Sadre and several of his family, but the larger clerical system and their mosques survived. Consequently, the mosques became the only avenue through which dissent could continue.

In postwar Iraq, the Shi'a clergy led by the Iranian-born Ayatollah Sistani, urged their followers to participate in "free" elections and to support the process toward the ratification and implementation of a new Iraqi constitution. Given that about 60 percent of the Iraqi population is Shi'a Muslim, and given the large-scale participation of the Shi'a population in elections, there was little doubt that so-called "democratic" procedures will lead to a Shi'a dominated elected government. But what will this mean for the future of Iraq?

The long-term prospect of democracy is better in Iraq than it is in Iran, because in Iraq the Shi'a clergy are forced to accommodate the large Kurdish and Sunni minorities. Also, so far there is no Ayatollah Khomeini among senior Iraqi clergy, so that minimum tolerance for secular voices might be maintained, at least outside Shi'a regions of Iraq.

Awaiting the Islamic Reformation

I have argued that there are "prodemocracy" aspects of Shi'a Islam tradition that can constructively feed into programs to build democracies in Iran and Iraq.[58] However, this can only be achieved if and when Shi'a seminaries and mosques, and the promotion and demotion of Shi'a clerics is independent from government control. Such independence would allow Shi'a clerics, seminaries, and mosques to play a vital role as critics of government policies and as a control on misuse of government power.

Obviously there are limits to how well Shi'a clerics could play a role as a "corrective" to government abuse, depending on the interpretation of Islam that clerics adopt. Within the community of Shi'a clerics, there is considerable diversity of views, and the current hegemony of fundamentalists will eventually give way to more progressive interpretations of Islam. The case of Khomeini demonstrates that Shi'a clerics do change their interpretations. For example, in the 1960s Khomeini opposed giving voting rights to women. After the revolution, he accepted votes for women. Making the *Koran* readily available in Farsi and other local languages, changing inheritance and marriage laws (to forbid polygamy and the practice of "temporary wives," for example), allowing women to serve as judges and to enjoy equality in the political and legal systems ... these are just some of the areas in which reforms will take place in the twenty-first century.

One way in which such reforms will become more likely is if more progressive ayatollahs emerge in the historically important Shi'a centers of Najaf and Karbala, Iraq. Recall from our earlier discussion that historically, the leading Shi'a clergy were centered in Najaf and Karbala in Iraq, out of direct reach of government authorities in Iran. Given freedom and resources to grow again, the seminaries in Najaf and Karbala could once more become the world centers of Shi'a learning, and attract the best and brightest Shi'a scholars from around the world.

Out of reach of the fundamentalist mullahs in Iran, progressive ayatollahs in Najaf and Karbala (Iraq) could attract a wide international following among the Shi'a faithful. Such progressive ayatollahs could use their influence to shape events toward greater freedom in Shi'a societies.

We are witnessing an indication of these possible future trends in the relationship between Kurds in Iraq and Kurds in Iran. The semi-independent and relatively democratic nature of Kurdish Iraq is looked at with admiration and envy by Kurds in Iran. The economic prosperity and political and social freedoms of Kurdish Iraq is attracting young, talented, Kurds from Iran to cross the border and seek work in Iraq. It is likely that the relative political freedom of Shi'a Iraq will attract leading progressive minds of Shi'a Islam from Ghom and other Iranian centers to Najaf and Karbala.

Such developments open up the possibility that modern democratic procedures and even institutions can be grafted onto "prodemocracy" aspects of Shi'a Islam. The resulting contextualized democracy would gain stability and solidity from deep, indigenous, and cultural foundations. Democracy based on these foundations would not on the surface look like American, or British, or French democracy, but at a deeper level it could still meet the central requirements for a democratic culture.

CONCLUDING COMMENT

One cannot be optimistic looking at the short-term prospects of the Near and Middle East. The gross mismanagement of postwar Iraq has immensely strengthened extremists in Iran and elsewhere. Iranian extremists have been handed what they themselves had failed to achieve in their eight-year-war with Saddam Hussein's regime: power and relative independence for a Shi'a theocracy in southern Iraq. British troops have stood aside while Islamic militia have enforced strict "moral" censorship, with the consequence that women once again have lost their place in the public sphere.

The new Iraqi constitution gives Iraqi Shi'a the power to monopolize Iraq's oil and establish an Islamic Republic in the south of Iraq, in practice if not in name. This development will further strengthen radicals in Iran and Iraq, and inspire violent Islamic movements and a morality supportive of terrorism around the world.

In this turmoil, local despots in Egypt, Saudi Arabia, Pakistan, and other Near and Middle Eastern countries are positioning themselves as "saviors of the West." The despots are sending a clear message to the West: either support us, or you will be faced with Islamic fundamentalist governments, like the one in Iran.

The best moral and political solution to this situation involves two strategies.

First, there is an urgent need for more detailed social and psychological assessments of Near and Middle Eastern societies, to identify local cultural characteristics that could serve as a foundation for democratic procedures and practices. As far as possible, "imported" democracy must be matched with these indigenous prodemocracy elements, even though from a Western perspective they might appear alien and bizarre. In the example of Shi'a Islam, I have argued that the traditional (in Iran, pre-1978) Shi'a seminary system, the method of the ascendance of clergy through the ranks, and the selection of a "source of emulation" by the faithful, is in some important respects democratic and allowing of voice and choice for the many.

A second important strategy for Western powers is to give greater support to secular opposition groups in the Near and Middle East, and stop supporting local dictators. In the long term, support for secular opposition and democracy weakens terrorism, whereas support for the ruling despots inflames terrorist movements. Georgia and Ukraine had some room for organized oppositions, so they evolved into some shape of democracy by 2005, with weak support for Islamic radicals. On the other hand, Uzbekistan has remained an absolute dictatorship with no room for organized, open, secular opposition, with the consequence that it has a much stronger Islamic radical movement. In Egypt, the secular opposition has been crushed, and so the fundamentalist Muslim Brotherhood is fast gaining ground and threatens to take over the country.

We must recognize that the Near and Middle Eastern dictatorships being propped up by the West are breeding, not helping to end, terrorism. After 9/11 the IRA came under intense pressure from different quarters, particularly key leaders in the United States, to abandon violence. Within months this pressure began to have effect, with the IRA declaring it had abandoned violence once and for all on July 28, 2005. The key to this change was the pressure from U.S. leaders. But it is only recently that Al Qaeda came to feel the same pressures from its key supporters in the leadership of Saudi Arabia and Pakistan. This pressure is not effective, because the political, social, economic, and cultural conditions of Saudi Arabia and Pakistan further strengthen the identity crisis being experienced by Muslims.

Fundamentalist Islam is on the rise in large part because it is the only movement and ideology being given room to offer a solution to the identity crisis being experienced by Islamic communities. This identity crisis is deep and pervasive, and so powerful that it motors fanatical movements and destructive terrorist organizations. The suicide bomber is driven by an urge that is even stronger than the will to live, and that is the will to live a meaningful life through an authentic identity. Unless we offer peaceful paths for people to find meaning, fulfillment, and authenticity, terrorism and the enormously costly war on terror will continue well into the twenty-first century.

APPENDIX

From the Terrorists' Point of View: Reflecting Back on American Culture

Other societies can serve as mirrors, allowing us to reflect back on ourselves and achieve a better understanding of our own lives and the narratives that guide us. There is a lot that needs to be understood in the case of America in the twenty-first century: How have so many monumental mistakes been made in foreign policy? Why has the management of postwar Iraq been so disastrous?

Those inclined to adopt purely political explanations will immediately jump to the conclusion that the answers to these questions have to do with the political party in power—the Republicans are to blame. Although a case can be made for holding the spotlight on inept Republican leaders in charge,[59] rather than dive into the political blame game, I focus on the far more subtle cultural processes that are common to American culture.

The manner in which the United States has carried out its foreign policy is influenced, sometimes explicitly, by aspects of American culture, and the particular narratives dominant in this culture. These narratives run through the American Dream, and are strongly reflected in classic Hollywood movies, such as that uniquely American art form, the cowboy movie.

To understand U.S. foreign policy, the "war on terror," and the behavior of the United States military in Iraq, it is necessary to step back and reflect on the nature of the larger culture back in the United States.

In the narratives that dominate this larger culture, *the hero has certain virtues that the community lacks*. The collective is to be distrusted, and all hope must rest on individual initiative and courage.

Second, *victory is assured to those individuals who possess particular heroic virtues*. There is only one possible ending to the American narrative: Victory.

THE SUPREMACY OF THE INDIVIDUAL OVER THE COMMUNITY

Time is running out for the battle-scarred sheriff. He thought he was free to start up a new life, a peaceful life, with his young bride, but trouble caught up with him just minutes after their wedding. The train arrives at noon, and it brings a gang of men intent on killing him. He could have left town, moved to a new place with his bride as previously planned, but he chose to stay and fight.

Time is running out. A gang of men will soon arrive to kill him, but he has no help. The entire town has turned its back on him. Every door he tries is slammed in his face. Each plea for help is shunned. The community is a coward. The collectivity has no backbone. The sheriff, played by Gary Cooper in *High Noon*, must fight alone.

Time has run out. The train has arrived. The evil gang is in town, a town whose citizens have enjoyed the protection of the sheriff but will do nothing to help him in his hour of need. In the end it is his young bride, played by the luminous Grace Kelly, who stands by his side and helps him to win the battle.

After defeating the bad guys, the sheriff is once more surrounded by supportive citizens. The streets are safe again and the town folk have come out of hiding to get on with their politics, gossip, and profit making. He shows his disdain for them by throwing his badge of office in the dirt and riding out of town, alone with his bride.

The Lone Cowboy

Gary Cooper, John Wayne, Clint Eastwood . . . the very sound of these names conjures up images of self-reliance, men who are willing to fight for what they believe is right, even if it means struggling against the odds and the defective collective on their own. These are individuals who possess strength of character, moral discipline, and other virtues that the community lacks. It is in Hollywood cowboy films that we find the most earthy and compelling examples of such men, representing the American ideal of the self-reliant, rugged individual. They typically play strong silent types, men who have few words to say, but think hard about right and wrong, then fight with all of their might for what they believe to be right.

The sheriff in *High Noon* goes through agonizing moments of doubt: What should he do? Should he leave town? Now that the citizens will not help him, is it worth staying to clean up the streets again? What about his young bride, what will become of her if he is killed only hours after their wedding? Throughout *High Noon*, the audience is keenly aware of the price paid by the sheriff for acting independently, going it alone.

The self-reliant individual is rational; he thinks first and only acts after he has come to a moral decision. But once Gary Cooper has made up his mind that the right thing to do is to stay and fight, then he acts. He gives his word, sometimes only to himself, and he acts on it. He stays true to an inner moral compos. He has the sincerity that Lionel Trilling identifies in *Sincerity and Authenticity* as having faded in the wider Western culture.

The Sheriff's fight in *High Noon* is ultimately a fight for his own dignity. It does not matter if the town people want him to stay or not. This fight is not about them; it is about a moral order that is much higher than them. It is about right and wrong, and the sheriff standing up for what he believes. It is his integrity as a self-contained, independent entity that is being upheld.

The cowboy film remains America's unique morality play. Good and bad are identified and the individual has to make a choice to fight on one side or the other. The choice is a personal one, made by an independent individual. In the American morality play, the heroic virtues of the self-contained individual and going it alone are idealized.

Urban Cowboys

It was a delightful autumn day and I was walking along New York City's Fifth Avenue. People rushed past, as I sauntered, lingered in front of luxurious shop windows, and wiled time away. I was early. I was to meet a former student at noon, but it was only 11:40 a.m. and I had already found our cramped meeting place, a slither of a side-street restaurant.

As I lingered and watched New Yorkers striding past, I tried to remember things about Samantha, the former student I was meeting. Her confidence was striking. When she asked me for letters of reference to support her application to business schools to study for an MBA, I asked her how many schools she was applying to. Only two top ones, she replied. I suggested she should apply to more, to increase her chances of acceptance. No, she replied, two will be sufficient, and it was. She got accepted to both schools.

Soon after graduating from business school, she moved to New York City, got married and had a child. She sent me a line or two periodically. The last one I received told me about her divorce. She wrote asking for advice about returning to graduate school to complete a Ph.D. She said she wanted greater intellectual challenges in her life. When she learned of my visit to New York City, she invited me to lunch.

Someone tapped me on the shoulder, and when I turned around Samantha was smiling in front of me. "Where is your traveling bag?" I asked, referring to a "lucky" backpack she used to have as a student. She traveled a lot in those days, and her backpack was covered with badges from many different countries. "I think I left it in Australia," she replied, launching into another story of how she had spent a summer gaining international work experience "Down Under." Over lunch, I learned more about her life during the last decade.

She was still in anguish about her marriage, which had failed despite the help she had sought from marriage guidance counselors and psychoanalysts. Both she and her husband had regular therapy sessions, and even her six-year-old child was in therapy. One of the criticisms she repeated of her husband was that he often missed his therapy sessions. "He would be full of good intentions when we made the appointments," she said, "but just did not show up for most sessions. He knew he was ruining our chances, our future together."

Their divorce had turned out to be a messier affair than she had expected, and now everything was in the hands of their lawyers. She had given her lawyer all the details and was waiting for a final resolution.

"But I thought your father and uncle are lawyers?" I asked.

She explained that they both still practice, but she would not hear of her family having anything to do with her divorce.

She methodically discussed each of her challenges (she used the word "challenge" a lot), and next we turned to think about the financing of her Ph.D. She had worked with her accountant to formulate a budget plan. She had enough money to maintain her present life style during her studies, as long as she finished within four years. I explained some scholarship possibilities, and she said she would definitely apply and also pass the information to her accountant.

All through lunch there was something I wanted to ask, and I finally got the question out during the last few minutes of our meeting.

"What do your family think about all this?"

"My family?" She responded in a puzzled tone, "I would never let them interfere in my life. I love my family and friends, but I hire lawyers and accountants and therapists to solve my problems. They are the professionals, after all."

"Besides," she added, "I can do it on my own."

Independence from Family, Escape from the Defective Collective

I had time to walk from the restaurant to my next appointment with an editor, and on the way I came across an elderly man sitting on the pavement. A younger man was standing over him, harassing him and preventing him from getting up. Was this a robbery? Was the younger man drunk? Did the older man need help? Nobody stopped to find out. People did not even change their pace as they maneuvered around them in that busy New York street.

Enormous changes have come about in the sense of duties city dwellers feel toward one another. Now, the first duty is to leave others alone, to let them live in their own ways. Reciprocally, others have a duty not to interfere in our lives.

Who is responsible for intervening when things go wrong? The experts, of course. There are now professionals specially trained to intervene in every kind of situation: Marriage counselors, psychoanalysts, psychiatrists, genetic therapists, social workers . . . and of course an array of lawyers. The list of experts seems endless. From buying clothes to taking holidays, from furnishing our homes to choosing a spouse, it seems that for every single area of life, no matter how narrow or seemingly intimate, there are multitudes of specialists.

We are ready to pour out in detail all of our personal histories and experiences to experts, but keep family and friends at a distance. The marriage guidance counselor and the therapist are told everything and entrusted with the most important decisions, but the "intrusion" of family and friends is not tolerated. Lawyers are permitted to dig into the most personal aspects of our private lives, but family and "intimate" friends are kept out. Our parents are not allowed to "meddle" in our affairs, but professional experts are given freedom to roam where they will and give opinions on the most secretive of our affairs.

If our spouses do not take advice from our family, they are forgiven, but if they do not abide by a therapist's rules, they are condemned.

The family and the community, once a rich repository of wisdom and knowledge, is kept at a distance and treated as a threat to the independence of individuals. Neighbors, friends, and family now have their roles confined within much narrower boundaries. They serve more specialized purposes, such as providing a supportive cast during special seasons (Christmas, Thanksgiving) and occasions (wedding celebrations, anniversaries, and birthdays). The increased personal space of individuals for family and community has created a vacuum, into which have rushed armies of specialists.

Specialists in Their New Roles in Support of Independent Individuals

Received wisdom tells us that specialists have achieved their pivotal positions through efficacy. They are efficient, whereas family and community members lack professional training and allow personal biases to guide their judgments and actions. The defense of expertise and the role of modern specialists would be more convincing if their record was better. In the political arena, Philip Tetlock's (2005) research shows that experts are generally no better than lay persons at making predictions about the course of events. In the legal arena, it is common wisdom that lawyers exacerbate rather than solve most disagreements. What begins as different points of view between neighbors and coworkers often turns into contentious law cases, blown out of proportion by the profit motive in law firms.

Perhaps lawyers are too easy a target for such criticism? But so are therapists, marriage counselors, and scores of others expert groups. Most people who receive help from therapists (psychoanalysts, clinical psychologists, and so on) would have the same chances of recovery if they went about their lives without resort to professional therapy. As for marriage counselors, the 50 percent divorce rate for first marriages and 60 percent for second marriages does not seem to indicate a high success rate for them.

The argument that "things could be worse without us experts" brings the natural counter, "they might also be better without you."

Nor is it a good argument to claim that complexity makes specialists essential: Why should choosing the color of our clothes require "expertise"? Hundreds of self-help books offer expert guidance for the most mundane and trivial areas.

Of course without some modern experts our technologically advanced societies would collapse. Our computers would crash and our lives would become shorter and more brutish. Medical experts save lives and relieve suffering. But even in medicine, we have exaggerated the objectivity of experts and put them on pedestals. As Lynn Payer points out in *Medicine and Culture*, the practice of medicine is far from objective.

Like all other human enterprises, medicine is influenced by cultural biases. American medicine is aggressive, meaning that compared to the treatment they receive in other Western societies, patients in America are more likely to be operated on, to be administered medication, and to receive higher doses of drugs. Doctors often justify their much higher rates of cesarean sections, hysterectomies, and the like, by answering they must treat more aggressively or they will be sued for malpractice. This is a prime example of how the intrusion of experts, in this case lawyers, into every crevice of American society has changed professional and personal lives.

Choosing Who We Rely on in A Free Market

The blatant cultural biases shown by even the most "scientific" groups of specialists, such as medical doctors, suggests that modern specialists have not achieved their pivotal positions through objectivity alone. We do not divulge our personal secrets to marriage guidance counselors, lawyers, and others, rather than to family and friends, because of a supposed objectivity advantage. Another, more subtle explanation works better, one that links personal lives to notions about independence and freedom in the open market.

Family and community can box us in, but specialists allow each of us more room to maneuver. They can be hired and fired. Relationships with lawyers and therapists do not involve long-term commitment, they imply freely selecting services in an open market. Individuals do not seem tied down by such relationships; they seem to remain free to move on, to select another specialist, to keep looking beyond to a seemingly open horizon—particularly when people are motivated to continue seemingly endless "treatments."

Surgical Attacks

The same narratives that explain and guide the intrusion of experts into the most intimate relationships in American lives, explain and guide the "surgical attacks" on targets in Iraq since the American-led invasion of 2003. Just as expert dissection and incision is part of the unraveling of family relations in America, it is now part of the unraveling of Iraqi society.

The American-led invasion of Iraq was to be conducted by a leaner, smaller, expert military. "Pinpoint bombing," "targeted attacks," "precise incisions" . . . the language of expertise was used to describe how the new military would operate on the body of Iraqi society, neatly cut and nullify the cancerous enemy, disinfect the body, and leave it clean and healthy. A smaller military would be needed, because expertise requires a highly skilled, technologically advanced elite.

Psychiatrists, lawyers, political and military experts, these groups can all take an objective, hands-off approach. They are not like family and friends, who become emotionally involved. Experts stand at a distance, as they weave us through divorce proceedings; just as the lean "expert" military does not get involved as precise incisions are made and "cancerous cells" are cut out of the Iraqi population. The blood and tears have to be dealt with professionally, objectively, at a distance.

Experts do their jobs and move on, untouched and independent. Therapists and lawyers bring an end to divorce cases, neatly separate families, and move on. The expert, lean military completes precision, surgical attacks, cleans up the body of society, and moves on. Expertise allows for detachment and independence. After a few short weeks, victory is declared and Iraqi society is now "safer for democracy."

High Noon Revisited

The Sheriff in *High Noon* could only stay true to himself by moving on, remaining independent. Like so many cowboy movies, *High Noon* ends with the hero riding out of town, merging with a distant but unreachable horizon. The constantly moving hero is ahead of the crowds, the "good" citizens, always part of a moving frontier. We get the strong sense in *High Noon* that if the Sheriff did not ride out of town, he would fail on a mission much more important than saving the town.

Modern Americans also try to remain true to themselves, they also strive for sincerity. In the 1960s, many were drawn to a path sketched out by Henry Thoreau and other American transcendentalists. This path involved simplifying life in order to get at its essentials. "I went to the woods because I wished to live deliberately," Thoreau wrote (1854–1983, p. 135), "to front only the essential facts of life, and see if I could not learn what it had to teach, and not, when I came to die, discover that I had not lived. I did not wish to live what was not life."

But Thoreau's path was only followed by most American's in daydreams; the flower power generation backpacked to California and India, but soon melted into the mainstream of society. Thoreau's did not prove to be a practical path to follow for citizens in technologically advanced societies. Explorations of Mars and the "final frontier" of space proved far more appealing than meditation in the woods.

Although Americans could not be true to themselves and to "what life is" using Thoreau's formula, their desire for sincerity lingers. It is in this connection that we can better understand their relationships with family and community on the one hand, and with specialists on the other. Being true to oneself in modern America has come to mean being independent, mobile, and self-reliant. Specialists make this possible, because they enable individuals to satisfy their needs without sacrificing independence.

The services of specialists can be bought, used, and terminated as needed, without long-term relationships and commitments. One specialist can be replaced by another in the time it takes to refer to a telephone directory and complete a call. Individuals can "be themselves" and make themselves according to their abilities and tastes, without being hampered by the inherited baggage of family and community. Expert interventions, like surgical strikes, are supposed to guarantee autonomy and detachment; they are to provide technical solutions to moral problems, making the twenty-first century American military "objective, precise, scientific" and somehow outside the moral domain. But sincerity is not to be regained this way. Some relationships cannot be broken without deepening cuts, some interventions require bonding before healing can take place.

TSARINAS, ROCKY, AND VICTORY ASSURED

He is an outsider, a nobody, just another neighborhood bum who unexpectedly gets a shot at the big time. His life is ordinary, the girl he loves is ordinary, and even his American Dream is ordinary—to make it big, to climb up the ladder of success.

Suddenly, Rocky gets that chance, in a way that is both unexpected and expected, in a way that is scripted in the American Dream narrative, but yet is a surprise twist in how the narrative plays out this particular time. The world heavyweight boxing champion needs a walkover victory, a "filler-fight," something he can do while the promoters and big wheelers of the boxing world prepare him for the next multimillion dollar *fight of the century* against an opponent who "really" matters. In the mean time, they give Rocky the honor of being stomped on by the champ.

But Rocky the underdog is not about to roll over and die. He grabs for his role as hero in the American Dream narrative, digs deep, and inspires himself to make a success of the one and only real break, the one in a million chance, which fortune has thrown his way—and which, we imagine, fortune throws in the way of everyone, once in a lifetime on American streets.

Rocky begins to act out his big dreams, to put dormant plans into action. He can do it, this unknown boxer can beat the world champion and become a somebody. He can slip through the momentary crack that has miraculously opened up for him, and make a grab for the big prize. Rocky the boxer has all of America rooting for him, he can make the American Dream come alive, and he can show that the road to success is still open to underdogs. Victory is assured for Rocky and other individuals who possess the key heroic virtues. They cannot be defeated—rather like Superman and the other action heroes.

Interwoven with the story of Rocky the local boxer set in Philadelphia is the story of Sylvester Stallone, the unlikely dramatist who makes it big time in Hollywood. Until Rocky, Stallone had been a small-time actor and a would-be screenwriter. Success, almost unfathomable box-office success, came with Rocky. Although Stallone never managed to win respect for his writing, or develop an image as a "serious" actor, his financial success was record-breaking. The original Rocky was followed by multiple sequels, and the Rambo series made him hundreds of millions more. The public witnessed the American Dream of rags to riches success both on the screen and off, both with the heroes Stallone created and with himself.

Stallone was blessed with all the disadvantages required for a person to fully play out the American Dream. Born into an ethnic family (he was nicknamed the "Italian stallion") of modest means, he did not do well at school. By the time he was twenty years old he had all the signs of being a marginal, a failure. No education, no money, and little prospects. Thus, his later success was all the more spectacular, and all the more an endorsement of the American system. If this guy can make it, anyone can! This success shows that American society really is open, that anyone can make it if they follow the dream.

The narrative of the American Dream has only one ending: victory. The individual with the right combination of virtues can only fulfill the dream, just as America on the world stage can only arrive at manifest destiny. Like a boxer who must always be declared the winner, America follows one and only story line.

Stallone is at the first stage of the American Dream success story. He is the one who establishes a dynasty. Like Henry Ford I, he has made the breakthrough. But which way from here? What can successful American dynasties become?

The Tsarinas

As I turn a corner and walk into the small museum restaurant, the portrait suddenly appears. It is hanging in front of the entrance, impossible to miss. The pose is imperial, the facial expression regal. The middle-aged lady could be a European queen, an empress, or a tsarina. Yes, a tsarina. The Fabergé eggs and other icons from Russia suggest a tsarina.

This is the American heiress Mary Weather Post: She is at the other end of the American Dream from Rocky; he is at the start of the race, and she has passed the finishing tape. She inherited the Post family fortune, as well as an aristocratic life style. When she visited Russia, she bought heaps of Russian jewelry and art to fill her mansions back in America. One of her homes in Washington, D.C. is now a museum, and it is here that I stand, mesmerized by her portrait, the one in which her true identity is revealed as a tsarina.

Mary Weather Post does not just look like a tsarina, she is a tsarina, with estates and mansions and crown jewels. We, the thousands who stream through her former homes to gaze at her treasures and trinkets, are not like her subjects, we are her subjects. She casts an aloof eye on us—we who are removed from her world by several generations of stupendous wealth and fame.

Having escaped from the Old World of Europe, with its class system and ancient aristocracies, Americans advertised their society as a true meritocracy, a place where the only thing that matters is individual efforts and talents. The American Dream enfolds alluring narratives in the context of an open society where individuals can move up and down the status hierarchy depending on personal characteristics; a place where underdogs can rise to the top, as long as they practice self-help and individual responsibility. Rocky is the realization of this dream.

But where does the road lead to? What do successful Americans become? They become Mary Weather Post. They become tsarinas and tsars. They become absorbed into the Western aristocracy. They do not emulate English, French, or Russian aristocracies; they become them.

Rocky is American, Mary Weather Post is European; in the American Dream, the road to success is American, the end of the road is European.

Only Future Success Matters

"Who is he?" I demanded, "Do you know?"
"He's just a man named Gatsby."
"Where is he from, I mean?" (1925, p. 49)

Why is F. Scott Fitzgerald's *The Great Gatsby* the quintessential American story? Is it Gatsby's enigmatic past? Is it the experience of the present as tiresome and anxiety ridden? No, it is the inspiration of future success, in this case the dream Gatsby has of an imagined perfection achieved in life with Daisy, which marks this story as American. Gatsby's intense faith in the future, and his utter belief that events will eventually turn his way and allow him to fulfill his dreams, is a continually repeated theme in the larger American narrative. The hero is assured victory, because he has the individual characteristics needed to succeed.

In this American narrative, the hero always leads the cavalry to arrive on time to win the war, even if sometimes American forces face temporary defeat in a battle. The image of John Wayne riding in at the head of the Texas cavalry to drive away the marauding Indians is blazed across the American imagination, whether that imagination is crafting Hollywood movies or foreign policy.

I was reminded of this recently when I talked with a group of American foreign policy experts about different "hot spots" in the world. There were many differences between situations in the various political "hot spots," but there was also one underlying similarity. Again and again, the American experts constructed narratives that involved the equivalent of John Wayne riding in with the cavalry and bringing a glorious and happy end to hostilities. There were only happy endings for the American side—and the "marauding Indians" were often allowed to suffer an unhappy fate.

But what happens when reality does not fit this American narrative? What happens when John Wayne and the cavalry arrive too late, or are unable to defeat the enemy? What next, when the hero fails to win victory? How is a Vietnam scenario taken into consideration?

The answer is that a Vietnam scenario is not taken into consideration and the American narrative only plans for victory. This tendency has been bolstered by the demise of the Soviet Union, with the result that the United States is now the sole superpower—and surely a superpower can only experience victory?

The "victory narrative" even comes to the forefront when Americans consider the future of remote political "hot spots," such as Taiwan. I recently witnessed a group of American foreign policy experts discuss a variety of possible scenarios for the future of Taiwan. Most of the scenarios involved conflict, from localized skirmishes to multinational wars, involving China and the United States, with Japan and other nations as supporting cast. Although there were many different scenarios, one stark common theme stood out: John Wayne and the U.S. cavalry would charge onto the scene and the movie would end with an American victory. For the American experts, it was inconceivable that the cavalry would not save the day, just as it had been inconceivable that John Wayne and the cavalry could lose control of events in Iraq after the 2003 invasion.

When the Victory Narrative Meets an Ambiguous Ending

> Mulla's nerves were on edge.
> "Why don't you go for a walk?" his wife asked him.
> Immediately Mulla left the house and walked for two days until he met a fellow walking in the opposite direction.
> "Will you do me a favor?" Mulla asked the stranger.
> "Of course, what can I do for you?"
> "When you reach my house ask my wife if I have walked far enough."
>
> (Nakosteen, 1974, p. 55)

In the final scene of *Shane*, the archetypical western movie, the hero is shown riding out of town and into the mountains, wounded and alone. Although the destination and future adventures of Shane are unknown, one thing is unambiguous: the good guys have won another fight. The bad guys in this case are the Riker brothers, ranch owners who hire a professional gunslinger to drive the smaller farmers out of the valley. But

Shane steps in and defeats both the gunslinger and the Riker brothers, freeing up the valley for the good farmers.

There are two ways in which Shane and other cowboy movies are unambiguous. First, the fight between good and evil has closure. Second, the good guys always win. President Bush was acting according to this narrative when he stood on a U.S. warship with "Mission Accomplished" brandished high in the background immediately after the invasion of Iraq in 2003. But by now the world has recognized that the "war on terror" does not fit the victory narrative of cowboy movies—it seems to better fit with the narratives of Mulla Nasreddin, used by Sufi teachers to impart wisdom. How far is far enough for the Mulla to walk?

How long is a "war on terror" supposed to last?

What does "Mission Accomplished" mean in the narrative of the "war on terror"?

How does an army fight a war when the enemy, the "other side", remains unknown?

How does a government bring a war to conclusion when the leaders of the other side cannot be found?

What does "victory" mean in this new war—the annihilation of most terrorists? Some terrorists? All terrorists?

Where is the battlefield? Is it Iraq? The Near East? Asia? Africa? Europe? All the rest of the world outside the United States?

But, of course, the battlefield must include the United States, because that is the prime target of both sides in the "war on terror."

Perhaps inevitably, it is also in the United States that the most important changes have come about because of the "war on terror." Critics of U.S. government policy, and particularly defenders of human rights, are now routinely accused of giving "comfort to the enemy" and "letting the troops down." The U.S. government has felt compelled to do whatever it takes, including wiretapping without court approval, detention without legal representation, and even torture (according to international standards accepted by most legal experts and organizations such as *Amnesty International*), to gain the upper hand in the "war on terror."

Can one be a defender of human rights if it becomes "necessary" to torture prisoners in order to defend human rights? Can one establish a democracy if in order to establish that democracy it becomes "necessary" to set aside democratic procedures? If we accept the general principle that the ends do not justify the means, are we justified in making exceptions? What if it is only through exceptions that we can bring about the conditions necessary for us to put into practice the principle that the ends do not justify the ends?

So far, the U.S. government has not addressed such questions in a satisfactory way on the stage of world public opinion. As criticism from abroad has increased, and the drum beat of the "war on terror" has continued, pressures on people to conform and to obey inside the United States have also increased.

Many of the policies adopted by the U.S. government are predictable on the basis of a universal relationship between threat from outside a group and processes inside the group: External threat inevitably results in some measure of internal repression, the rise of aggressive leadership, as well as displacement of aggression onto minorities and particular outgroups. Freedom and human rights are the second casualties of war, after truth is first crucified. No doubt people will look back at this period in American history as they now look back judgmentally and with disappointment at the internment of Japanese–Americans in the United States during the Second World War.

REFERENCES

Fitzgeral, F. S. (1925). *The great gatsby.* New York: Charles Scribner's Sons.

Gordon, M. R., and Trainor, B. E. (2006). *Cobra II: The inside story of the invasion and occupation of Iraq.* New York: Pantheon.

Nakosteen, M. (1974). *Mulla's donkey & other friends.* Boulder, CO: University of Colorado Libraries.

Payer, L. (1988). *Medicine and culture.* New York: Penguin Books.

Tetlock, P. (2005). *Expert political judgment: How good is it? How do we know?* Princeton, NJ: Princeton University Press.

Thoreau, H. D. (1854/1983). *Walden and civil disobedience.* Harmondsworth, UK: Penguin.

Trilling, L. (1971). *Sincerity and authenticity.* Cambridge, MA: Harvard University Press.

NOTES

CHAPTER 1

1. Rice urges Egyptians and Saudis to democratize. *New York Times*, pp. 1 and 4, June 21, 2005.

2. Weiner, 2005.

CHAPTER 2

3. The major theories are discussed in Taylor and Moghaddam (1994), and Brown and Gaertner (2001).

4. For a more detailed outline of Terror Management Theory, see Pyszczynski, Solomon, and Greenberg (2003).

5. Dawkins (1989).

6. Daly and Wilson (1988) provide detailed evidence to support the idea that adopted children are more likely to be injured and killed.

7. For a review of research in this area, see Hafer and Bègue (2005).

8. Jost, Banaji, and Nosek (2004) provide a useful review of the research on the System Justification Theory.

9. This cycle of focus by revolutionaries on rights when in opposition, and on duties after they achieve power, is discussed in Moghaddam (2004b).

10. For a more detailed discussion of the Resource Mobilization Theory, see McCarthy and Wolfson (1996).

11. The primacy of collective consciousness and identity is discussed in Moghaddam (2003) and Taylor (2002).

12. One of the most illuminating studies on this theme is by Barker and Gump (1964).

CHAPTER 3

13. Language death is discussed in Crystal (2000).

14. For a more in-depth discussion of the self and self-esteem, see Baumeister (1999).

15. I first discussed the staircase metaphor in Moghaddam (2005b).

CHAPTER 4

16. The extent of Osama bin Laden's wealth was exaggerated in the popular media. See Halliday (2005).

17. Coogan (2002) provides a highly insightful account of the IRA.

18. There is evidence to suggest that we see many different types of things as impacting the group more than it does us, see Moghaddam, Stolkin, and Hutcheson (1997).

CHAPTER 5

19. Plato, *The Republic*, Book Three, 415b, c, d.

20. Brosnan and de Waal (2003).

21. An example of research on culture among animals is in Schaik, C. P. van., Ancrenaz, M., Borgon, G., Galdikas, B., Knott, C. D., Singleton, I., Suzuki, A., Utami, S. S., and Merrill, M. (2003). Orangutan cultures and the evolution of material culture. *Science*, 299: 102–105.

22. Dershowitz (2004).

23. Chagnon, 1997, p. 179.

24. Hart, Pilling, and Goodale (2001) provide a concise and very readable account of the Tiwi.

25. Sen (1999) is among the leading thinkers to explore the relationship between choice, material growth, and development.

26. Ehrlich and Ehrlich (2004) present a convincing picture of how our misdirected environmental policies are limiting our future.

CHAPTER 6

27. See the views of leading evangelical Christians in Cooperman (2002).

CHAPTER 7

28. Lorenz (1966).

29. Searles and Berger (1995).

30. But there are some ways in which the United States is exceptional; see chapter 4 in Moghaddam (2002).

31. For data on income inequalities within nations, see the United Nations Human Development Report (2004), at http://www.unstats.un.org. There is also

a heated debate about global income inequalities, see Firebaugh and Goesling (2004) and Wade (2004).

32. Sageman (2004) presents an insightful analysis of the role of social networks in terrorism.

33. Hart et al. (2001).

34. For a summary of this research, see chapter 15 in Moghaddam (2005a).

CHAPTER 8

35. Bodansky (2001) provides an authoritative profile of bin Laden. In this section, I have tried to provide readily accessible sources for each example I give of the different terrorist specializations.

36. For a discussion of Al Qaeda and the role of Zawahiri and other notable terrorist figures, see Alexander and Swetman (2002).

37. Glanz (2005).

38. Coll and Glasser (2005).

39. The 9/11 Commission Report (2004) gives a good account of Atta's role. See also McDermott (2005).

40. Ismail (2005).

41. Aizenman (2005).

42. Fattah (2005).

43. Bonner (2005).

CHAPTER 9

44. Sherif (1936).

45. Asch (1956).

46. Berns et al. (2005).

47. Goffman (1961).

48. Zimbardo (1972). This simulation study by Zimbardo is a wonderful example of how research can become highly influential, without meeting the traditional "scientific" criteria and without being published in mainstream scientific journals.

49. Janis (1972).

50. Milgram (1974).

51. Mainstream psychology has mistakenly adopted a causal model for all thought and action, and implicitly or explicitly abandoned intentionality. But only some types of thought and action can be adequately explained causally; other types require a normative explanation, integral to which is intentionality (see Moghaddam, 2002).

52. See Pape (2005). Other insightful books on suicide terrorism are Bloom (2005) and McDermott (2005).

CHAPTER 10

53. See Moghaddam (2002), particularly pages 29–34.

54. Psychologists have given little attention to the psychological requirements for democracy, for some exceptions see Sullivan and Transue (1999) and Tetlock (1998).

55. Tyler and Huo (2002) present an excellent case for the importance of procedural justice and the involvement of citizens.

56. For discussions on democracy, culture, and Islam, see Hunter and Malik (2005); Kim, Aasen, and Ebadi (2003); Price (1999); and Sadiki (2004).

57. See Arjomand (1988). For a broader discussion of this "stability within change," see Moghaddam and Crystal (1997).

58. For broader discussions of the so-called Islamic reformation, see Browers and Kurzman (2003).

APPENDIX

59. For example, the analysis of Gordon and Trainor, 2006, highlights the repeated and continued miscalculations of Donald Rumsfeld during the 2003 invasion and subsequent occupation of Iraq by American led forces.

SELECTED BIBLIOGRAPHY

Aburish, S. K. (1995). *The rise, corruption, and coming fall of the House of Saud.* New York: St. Martin's Press.

Aizenman, N. C. (2005). I will go to do jihad again and again. *The Washington Post*, August 21, A17.

Alexander, Y. (2002). *Palestinian religious terrorism: Hamas and Islamic jihad.* Ardsley, NY: Transnational Publishers.

Alexander, Y., and Swetman, M. (2002). *Osama bin Laden's Al-Qaida: Profile of a terrorist network.* Ardsley, NY: Transnational Publishers.

Altemeyer, B. (1988). *Enemies of freedom: Understanding right-wing authoritarianism.* San Francisco: Jossey-Bass.

Arjomand, A. A. (1988). *The turban for the crown.* New York: Oxford University Press.

Asch, S. E. (1956). Studies of independence and conformity: A minority of one against a unanimous majority. *Psychological Monographs, 70* (9, No. 416).

Atran, S. (2003). Genesis of suicide terrorism. *Science, 299,* 1534–1539.

Bandura, A. (2004). The role of selective moral disengagement in terrorism and counterterrorism. In F. M. Moghaddam and A. J. Marsella (Eds.), *Understanding terrorism: Psychosocial roots, causes, and consequences* (pp. 121–150). Washington, D.C.: American Psychological Association Press.

Barker, R. G., and Gump, P. V. (1964). *Big school, small school: School size and student behavior.* Stanford, CA: Stanford University Press.

Baumeister, R. F. (Ed.) (1999). *Self in social psychology.* New York: Psychology Press.

Bernholz, P. (2004). Supreme values as the basis for terror. *European Journal of Political Economy, 20,* 317–333.

Berns, G. S., Chappelow, J., Zink, C. F., Pagnoni, G., and Martin-Skurski, M. E. (2005). Neurobiological correlates of social conformity and independence during mental rotation. *Biological Psychiatry, 58*, 245–253.

Bloom, M. (2005). *Dying to kill: The allure of suicide terror.* New York: Columbia University Press.

Bodansky, Y. (2001). *Bin Laden: The man who declared war on America.* New York: Random House.

Bonner, R. (2005). Bali suicide bombers said to have belonged to small gang. *The New York Times,* October 7, A3.

Booth, K., and Dunne, T. (Eds.) (2002). *Worlds in collision: Terror and the future global order.* New York: Palgrave Mamillan.

Borum, R. (2004). *Psychology of terrorism.* Tampa, FL.: University of South Florida.

Brosnan, S. F., and de Waal, F. B. (2003). Monkeys reject unequal pay. *Nature, 425,* 297–299.

Browers, M., and Kurzman, C. (Eds.) (2003). *An Islamic reformation?* Lanham, MD: Lexington Books.

Brown, R., and Gaertner, S. L. (Eds.) (2001). *Blackwell handbook of social psychology: Intergroup processes.* Oxford: Blackwell.

Chagnon, N. (1997). *Yanomamo.* 5th ed. New York: Harcourt Brace.

Coll, S., and Glasser, S. B. (2005). Terrorists turn to the web as base of operations. *The Washington Post,* August 7, A1 and A16.

Coogan, T. P. (2002). *The IRA.* NewYork: Palgrave.

Cooper, H. H. A. (2001). The problem of definition revisited. *American Behavioral Scientist, 44,* 881–893.

Cooperman, A. (2002). Anti-Muslim remarks stir tempest. *The Washington Post,* June 20, A3.

Crenshaw, M. (2003). The causes of terrorism. In C. W. Kegley, Jr. (Ed.), *The new global terrorism: Characteristics, causes, controls.* Upper Saddle River, NJ: Prentice Hall.

Crystal, D. (2000). *Language death.* Cambridge: Cambridge University Press.

Daly, M., and Wilson, M. (1988). *Homicide.* New York: Aldine de Gruyter.

Danieli, Y., Brom, D., and Waizer, J. (Eds.) (2005). *The trauma of terror: Sharing knowledge and sharing care.* New York: Haworth Press. Davis, J. (2003). *Martyrs: Innocence, vengeance, and despair in the Middle East.* New York: Palgrove Macmillan.

Dawkins, R. (1989). *The selfish gene.* 2nd ed. Oxford: Oxford University Press.

Dershowitz, A. (2004). *Rights from wrongs: A secular theory of the origins of rights.* New York: Basic Books.

Ehrlich, P., and Ehrlich, A. (2004). *One with Nineveh: Politics, consumption, and the human future.* Washington, D.C.: Shearwater Press.

Ehrlich, P. R., and Liu, J. (2002). Some roots of terrorism. *Population and Environment, 24,* 183–191.

Fattah, H. M. (2005). Jordan arrests Iraqi woman in hotel blasts. *The New York Times,* November 14, A1 and A9.

Fields, R. M., Elbedour, S., and Hein, F. A. (2002). The Palestinian suicide bomber. In C. E. Stout (Ed.), *The psychology of terrorism* (Vol. 2, pp. 193–223). Westport, CT: Praeger.

Firebaugh, G., and Goesling, B. (2004). Accounting for the recent decline in global income inequality. *American Journal of Sociology*, *110*, 283–312.

Freud, S. (1921). Group psychology and the analysis of the ego. In J. Strachey (Ed. and trans.), *The standard edition of the complete psychological works*. Vol. 18. London: Hogarth.

Freud, S. (1930). Civilization and its discontents. In J. Strachey (Ed. and trans.), *The standard edition of the complete psychological works*. Vol. 21. London: Hogarth.

Glanz, J. (2005). In Jordanian case, hints of Iraq jihad network. *The New York Times*, July 29, A1 and A9.

Goffman, E. (1961). *Asylums*. Harmondsworth, UK: Penguin.

Gold, D. (2003). *Hatred's kingdom: How Saudi Arabia supports the New Global Terrorism*. Washington, D.C.: Regnery Publishing Inc.

Grossman, D. (1995). *On killing: The psychological cost of learning to kill in war and society*. New York: Little, Brown.

Hafer, C., and Bègue, L. (2005). Experimental research on just-world theory: Problems, developments, and future challenges. *Psychological Bulletin*, *131*, 128–167.

Haliday, F. (2005). *100 Myths about the Middle East*. Berkeley: University of California Press.

Hart, C. W. M., Pilling, A. R., and Goodale, J. (2001). *The Tiwi of North Australia*. 3rd ed. Belmont, CA: Wadsworth.

Henderson, H. (2004). *Global terrorism*. 2nd ed. New York: Facts on File, Inc.

Horgan, J., and Taylor, M. (2003). *The psychology of terrorism*. London: Frank Cass & Co.

Hunter, S. T., and Malik, H. (Eds.) (2005). *Modernization, democracy, and Islam*. Westport, CT: Praeger.

Ismail, N. H. (2005). Schooled for jihad. *The Washington Post*, June 26, B1 and B4.

Janis, I. L. (1972). *Victims of groupthink: A psychological study of foreign-policy decisions and fiascoes*. Boston: Houghton Mifflin.

Jost, J. T., Banaji, M. R., and Nosek, B. A. (2004). A decade of system justification theory: Accumulated evidence for conscious and unconscious bolstering of the status quo. *Political Psychology*, *25*, 881–919.

Kim, U., Aasen, H. S., and Ebadi, S. (Eds.) (2003). *Democracy, human rights, and Islam in modern Iran*. Bergen, Norway: Fagbokforlaget.

Linenthal, E. T. (2001). *The unfinished bombing: Oklahoma City in American memory*. New York: Oxford University Press.

Lorenz, K. (1966). *On aggression* (M. Wilson, trans.). New York: Harcourt, Brace & World.

McCarthy, J. D., and Wolfson, M. (1996). Resource mobilization by local social movement organizations: Agency, strategy, and organization in the movement against drunk driving. *American Sociological Review*, *61*, 1070–1088.

McDermott, T. (2005). *Perfect soldiers: The hijackers—who they were, why they did it*. New York: HarperCollins.

Milgram, S. (1974). *Obedience to authority: An experimental view*. New York: Harper & Row.

Miller, N., Pederson, W. C., Earlywine, M., and Pollock, V. E. (2003). A theoretical model of triggered displaced aggression. *Personality and Social Psychology Review, 7,* 75–97.

Moghaddam, F. M. (1997). *The specialized society: The plight of the individual in an age of individualism.* Westport, CT: Praeger.

_____. (1998). *Social psychology: Exploring universals in social behavior.* New York: Freeman.

_____. (2002). *The individual and society: A cultural integration.* New York: Worth.

_____. (2003). Interobjectivity and culture. *Culture & Psychology, 9,* 221–232.

_____. (2004a). Cultural continuities beneath the conflict between radical Islam and pro-Western forces: The case of Iran. In Y. T. Lee, C. McCauley, F. M. Moghaddam and S. Worchel (Eds.), *The psychology of ethnic and cultural conflict* (pp. 115–132). Westport, CT: Praeger.

_____. (2004b). The cycle of rights and duties in intergroup relations: Interobjectivity and perceived justice reassessed. *New Review of Social Psychology, 3,* 125–130.

_____. (2005a). *Great ideas in psychology: A cultural and historical introduction.* Oxford: Oneworld.

_____. (2005b). The staircase to terrorism: A psychological exploration. *American Psychologist, 60,* 161–169.

Moghaddam, F. M., and Crystal, D. (1997). Revolutions, samurai, and reductions: Change and continuity in Iran and Japan. *Journal of Political Psychology, 18,* 355–384.

Moghaddam, F. M., and Marsella, A. J. (Eds.) (2004), *Understanding terrorism: Psychosocial roots, consequences, and interventions* (pp. 223–246). Washington, D.C.: American Psychological Association Press.

Moghaddam, F. M., Stolkin, A. J., and Hutcheson, L. S. (1997). A generalized personal/group discrepancy: Testing the domain specificity of a perceived higher effect of events on my groups than on myself. *Personality and Social Psychology Bulletin, 23,* 743–750.

Pape, R. A. (2005). *Dying to win: The strategic logic of suicide terrorism.* New York: Random House.

Pearlstein, R. M. (1991). *The mind of the political terrorist.* Wilmington, DE: Scholarly Resources.

Plato (1987). *The Republic.* (Desmond Lee, trans.). Harmondsworth, UK: Penguin.

Price, D. E. (1999). *Islamic political culture, democracy, and human rights.* Westport, CT: Praeger.

Pyszcznski, T., Solomon, S., and Greenberg, J. (2003). *In the wake of 9/11: The psychology of terror.* Washington, D.C.: American Psychological Association.

Rapoport, D. C. (Ed.) (2002). *Inside terrorist organizations.* 2nd ed. London: Frank Cass & Co.

Ruby, C. L. (2002). Are terrorists mentally deranged? *Analysis of Social Issues and Public Policy, 2,* 15–26.

Rushdie, S. (2002). Anti-Americanism has taken the world by storm. *The Guardian.* Retrieved http://www.guardian.co.uk/afghanistan/comment/story/0,11447,645579,00.html.

Sadiki, L. (2004). *The search for Arab democracy: Discourses and counter discourses.* London: Hurst.

Sageman, M. (2004). *Understanding terror networks.* Pennsylvania, PA: University of Pennsylvania Press.

Schwartz, S. (2002). *The two faces of Islam: The house of Saud from tradition to terror.* New York: Doubleday.

Schweitzer, G. E. (2002). *The faceless enemy: The origins of modern terrorism.* Cambridge, MA: Perseus Publishing.

Schweitzer, Y. (Ed.) (2005). *Female suicide terrorists.* Tel Aviv, Israel: Jaffe Center Publication.

Scranton, P. (Ed.) (2002). *Beyond September 11: An anthology of dissent.* London: Pluto Press.

Searles, P., and Berger, R. J. (Eds.) (1995). *Rape and society: Readings on the problem of sexual assault.* Boulder, CO: Westview Press.

Sen, A K. (1999). *Development as freedom.* New York: Knopf.

Seul, J. R. (1999). "Ours if the way of God": Religion, identity, and intergroup conflict. *Journal of Peace Research, 36,* 553–569.

Shapira, S. (2000). *Hizballah between Iran and Lebanon.* Tel Aviv, Israel: Kakibbutz Hameuchad.

Sherif, M. (1936). *The psychology of group norms.* New York: Harper.

Silke, A. (Ed.) (2003). *Terrorism, victims, and society: Psychological perspectives on terrorism and its consequences.* Hoboken, NJ: Wiley.

Singapore Ministry of Home Affairs (2003). White paper: The Jemaah Islamiyah arrests. January 9. At http://www2.mha.gov.sg.

Speckhard, A., Tarabrina, N., Krasnov, V., and Akhmedova, K. (2004). Observations of suicide terrorists in action: the Chechen terrorist takeover of a Moscow Theater. *Terrorism and Political Violence, 16,* 305–327.

Stout, C. E. (Ed.) (2002). *The psychology of terrorism.* 4 vols. Westport, CT: Praeger.

Sullivan, J. L., and Transue, J. E. (1999). The psychological underpinnings of democracy. *Annual Review of Psychology, 50,* 625–650.

Taylor, D. M. (2002). *The quest for identity.* Westport, CT: Praeger.

Taylor, D. M., and Moghaddam, F. M. (1994). *Theories of intergroup relations: International social psychological perspectives.* Westport, CT: Praeger.

Taylor, M. (1988). *The terrorist.* London: Brassey's Defence Publishers.

Tetlock, P. E. (1998). The ever-shifting psychological foundations of democratic theory: Do citizens have the right stuff? *Critical Review, 12,* 545–561.

The 9/11 Commission Report: Final report of the National Commission on terrorist attacks upon the United States. (2004). New York: Norton.

Tyler, T. R., and Huo, Y. J. (2002). *Trust in the law.* New York: Russell Sage Foundation.

United Nations Development Programme (2004). *Human development report 2002: Deepening democracy in a fragmented world*. New York: Oxford University Press.

Van Schaik, C. P., Ancrenaz, M., Borgen, G., Galdikas, B., Knott, C. D., Singleton, I., et al. (2003). Orangutan cultures and the evolution of material culture. *Science, 299*, 102–105.

Wade, R. (2004). Is globalization reducing poverty and inequalities? *World Development, 32*, 567–589.

Weiner, T. (2005). Case of Cuban exile could test the U.S. definition of terrorism. *Washington Post*, May 9, A1 and A13.

Zimbardo, P. (1972). Pathology of imprisonment. *Transactional/Society*, 4–8 (a).

INDEX

About the Author

FATHALI M. MOGHADDAM, Professor of Psychology at Georgetown University, is an internationally known Iranian-born, British-educated psychologist with extensive research and consulting experience in intergroup conflict and terrorism. He previously held positions at McGill University and with the United Nations, and taught and researched in Iran for five years immediately after the 1978–79 revolution. His extensive publications include numerous books, among them books on the psychology of terrorism and ethnic and cultural conflict. His book *Understanding Terrorism: Psychosocial Roots, Consequences, and Interventions* (With A. J. Marsella) was selected by CHOICE (Current Reviews for Academic Libraries, American Library Association) as "A 2004 Outstanding Academic Title."